HOW
TO TORTURE
YOUR MIND

Books by Ralph L. Woods

America Reborn: A Plan for the Decentralization of Industry
Pilgrims' Places in North America: A Guide to Catholic Shrines
A Treasury of the Familiar
A Second Treasury of the Familiar
Behold the Man: An Anthology of Jesus Christ
The World of Dreams
A Treasury of Inspiration
The Businessman's Book of Quotations
A Treasury of Catholic Thinking
The Consolations of Catholicism
The Catholic Companion to the Bible
A Treasury of the Dog
A Treasury of Friendship
The Catholic Concept of Love and Marriage
The Family Reader of American Masterpieces
Famous Poems and the Little-Know Stories Behind Them
Poems of Prayer
The World Treasury of Religious Quotations
The Modern Handbook of Humor
Laurels for Fathers
Courage Is . . .
Faith Is . . .
Brotherhood Is . . .
A Treasury of Contentment

HOW TO TORTURE YOUR MIND

Paradoxes, Fallacies, Dilemmas, Figures, and Word Wonders

COMPILED AND EDITED BY

Ralph L. Woods

For the
Amusement of Amiable Cogitators

Funk & Wagnalls   NEW YORK

Grateful acknowledgment is made to the following publishers,
agents, and copyright owners for their cooperation in granting
permission for the use of material from the works indicated:

GEORGE ALLEN AND UNWIN LTD.: Bertrand Russell, *Nightmares
of Eminent People, The Scientific Outlook, Sceptical
Essays,* and *Mysticism and Logic;* P. E. B. Jourdain, *The
Philosophy of Bertrand Russell.*

AP NEWSFEATURES, New York: 1953 dispatch.

DMITRI A. BORGMANN, Oak Park, Illinois: six of his anagrams.

GEORGE BRAZILLER, INC.: Milic Čapek in J. T. Fraser, ed., *The
Voices of Time*

CAMBRIDGE UNIVERSITY PRESS, New York: Mc. T. E. McTag-
gart, *Nature of Existence,* C. D. Broad, ed. (1921); H. D.
P. Lee, *Zeno of Elea* (1936); A. S. Eddington, *Nature of
the Physical World* (1929).

CHILTON BOOK CO.: Paul Tabori, *The Art of Folly* (Copyright
© 1961 by Paul Tabori).

THOMAS Y. CROWELL: M. H. Greenblatt, *Mathematical Enter-
tainment* (Copyright © 1965 by M. H. Greenblatt).

DAWSON OF PALL MALL: Mary Mill Patrick, trans., *Sextus
Empiricus and Greek Skepticism* (including first book of
Pyrrhonic Sketches), published by Deighton Bell and Co.

DODD, MEAD AND CO.: Stephen Leacock, *My Remarkable Uncle
and Other Sketches* (Copyright 1942 by Dodd, Mead and
Co., Inc.).

iv

TO

Mona Thomas Woods

WHO ENJOYS THIS KIND OF THING

A little nonsense now and then

Is relished by the best of men.

—Anonymous

Preface

Years ago, in the course of library prowling. I sometimes encountered oddly interesting and amusing paradoxes, word tricks, sophisms, logical puzzles, and
illogical nonsense devised by great minds of the past.
I jotted down several of these and tried them on family
and friends. The resulting interest and amusement—
and sometimes heated controversy—planted the seed
from which this volume has sprung. I decided that if
a few casually gathered items could excite so much
interest and generate so much heat, then a carefully
selected and edited book containing a great variety of
paradoxes, sophisms, engimas, word tricks, logical
puzzles, and philosophical frivolities would unquestionably interest, amuse, and pleasantly perplex a great
many intelligent people.

The book's sole purpose is to amuse and divert readers with the intellectual acrobatics of some of the
more agile minds of the ages. Consequently, I have
readily excluded the technical jargon of the philosophers and the formidable terminology of the logicians
who propounded this brain bait.

Moreover, I have made no systematic attempt to
give the *possible* solutions of many of the paradoxes
and dilemmas. Here and there a solution has been
offered, but only when it was as interesting and read-
able as the paradox and dilemma itself.

Of course, many of the paradoxes and logical puzzles are considered insoluble, others are obviously and
intentionally absurd, some are fallacies resulting from
the misuse of ambiguous words, and still others are
of such a nature that the solutions suggested are de-

batable. The sophisms require no solution or explanation; they are simply amusing examples of what clever minds can devise to confuse, bewilder, and confound.

The large section of Word Wonders, Oddities, and Pen Pranks presents no real difficulties; the quirks, quips, and ingenuity therein are readily recognized and—hopefully—easily enjoyed.

It seems well for me to conclude with the reminder, however unnecessary it may be, that none of the solutions suggested is mine. This sort of thing amuses me immensely, but I would not dare to match wits with the adepts presented in these pages.

R. L. W.

Contents

Preface   ix

I   *Paradoxes, Dilemmas, and Other Problems*   3

II   *Logic and Illogic*   89

III   *Fun From Philosophers*   135

IV   *Math and Economics Guyed*   191

V   *Word Wonders, Oddities, and Pen Pranks*   255

Index   335

I

Paradoxes, Dilemmas, and Other Problems

1

Paradoxes, Dilemmas,
and Other Problems

Zeno's Paradox—

Achilles and the Tortoise

> Achilles can run ten times faster than the Tortoise. He therefore gives the Tortoise a hundred-yard start. While Achilles runs the first hundred yards, the Tortoise runs ten yards. While Achilles covers the ten yards, the Tortoise runs one yard. While Achilles is running that one yard, the Tortoise covers one-tenth of a yard, and so on ad infinitum.

Zeno of Elea used this paradox to prove there is no such things as motion. He argued that before Achilles could overtake the Tortoise he must first arrive at the point from which the Tortoise started. But during the time it took Achilles to reach the Tortoise's starting point, the Tortoise meanwhile would have advanced a certain distance, even though a shorter distance than covered by Achilles. Again, while Achilles covered the distance that the Tortoise advanced from its starting point, the Tortoise would have advanced another certain though proportionately shorter distance, and so on.

In short, during every period of time that Achilles covered distance already traversed by the Tortoise, the Tortoise would have advanced a yet further distance.

Even though the distances are continually decreasing ad infinitum, nevertheless Achilles would never overtake the Tortoise because of the infinite divisibility of magnitudes.

Simplicius upheld Zeno by arguing that any object in motion must first cover the first half of a distance, and then the whole distance. But before it covers that first half it must traverse half of half, and again half of that, and so on. Since halves are infinite in number because any length can be halved, it is therefore impossible to traverse an infinite number of positions in a finite time.

... And One Solution

The ambiguity of the word Infinite is the real fallacy in the amusing logical puzzle of Achilles and the Tortoise, a puzzle which has been too much for the ingenuity or patience of many philosophers, and among many others of Sir William Hamilton, who considered the sophism insoluble; as a sound argument, though leading to a palpable falsehood; not seeing that such an admission would be a *reductio ad absurdum* of the reasoning faculty itself. The fallacy, as Hobbes hinted, lies in the tacit assumption that whatever is infinitely diminished is infinite; but the following solution (to the invention of which I have no claim) is more precise and satisfactory.

The "forever" in the conclusion [i.e., that Achilles may run forever without overtaking the tortoise] means, for any length of time that can be supposed; but in the premises "ever" does not mean any length of time; it means any *number of subdivisions* of time. It means that we may divide a thousand feet by ten, and that quotient again by ten, and so on as often as we please; that there never needs be an end to the subdivisions of distance, nor consequently to those of the time in which it is performed. But an unlimited number of subdivisions may be made of that which is itself limited. The argument proves no other infinity of duration than may be embraced within five minutes. As long as the five minutes are not expired, what remains of them may be divided by ten, and again by ten, as often as we like, which is perfectly compatible with their being only five minutes altogether. It proves, in short, that to pass through this finite space requires a time which is infinitely divisible, but not an infinite time; the confounding of which distinction Hobbs had already seen to be the gist of the fallacy.

—JOHN STUART MILL

You Had Better Bet on Achilles

It has been said that if Achilles is to catch the more leisurely tortoise, he will have to occupy *more* positions than the tortoise in the same elapsed period of time. Since this is manifestly impossible, you may put your money on the tortoise.

But don't be too hasty. In fact, you had better bet on Achilles after all, for he is likely to win the race. Even though he may not have realized it, we have just finished proving that he could not overtake the tortoise by showing that a line a millionth of an inch long has just as many points as a line stretching from the earth to the furthest star. In other words, the points on the tiny line segment can be placed in one-to-one correspondence with the points on the great line, for there is no relation between the number of points on a line and its length. But this reveals the error in thinking that Achilles cannot catch the tortoise. The statement that Achilles must occupy as many distinct positions as the tortoise is correct. So is the statement that he must travel a greater distance than the tortoise in the same time. The only incorrect statement is the inference that since he must occupy the same number of positions as the tortoise he cannot travel further while doing so. Even though the classes of points on each line which correspond to the several positions of both Achilles and the tortoise are equivalent, the line representing the path of Achilles must travel further than the tortoise without successively touching more points.

—EDWARD KASNER AND JAMES NEWMAN

What the Tortoise Said to Achilles at the End of Their Race

Achilles had overtaken the Tortoise and had seated himself comfortably on its back.

"So you've got to the end of our race-course?" said the Tortoise. "Even though it does consist of an infinite series of distance? I thought some wiseacre or other had proved that the thing couldn't be done."

"It can be done," said Achilles. "It has been done! *Solvitur ambulando.* You see the distances were constantly diminishing, and so—"

"But if they had been constantly *increasing?*" the Tortoise interrupted. "How then?"

"Then I shouldn't be *here*," Achilles modestly replied. "And *you* would have been several times round the world by this time!"

—LEWIS CARROLL

Mathematicians finally put an end to all this amusing nonsense by figuring out that Achilles would overtake the tortoise 1,111-⅑ feet from his starting point.

6

Legend has it that one day Zeno proposed his paradox of motion—that you cannot travel an infinite number of points in a finite time—to Diogenes the Cynic. When Zeno had completed his statement, Diogenes silently got to his feet and walked away, to refute Zeno simply by moving. But Zeno was undisturbed; he said that things only *appear* to move, whereas logic proves that they cannot move. If one's senses tell one the contrary, then so much the worse for the senses.

This story is slightly spoiled by the best records that indicate Zeno died fourteen years before Diogenes was born.

The Arrow In Flight Is At Rest

Simplicius argues that an arrow in flight is at rest because any object in motion occupies a space equal it itself, and that which occupies a space equal to itself is not in motion. Therefore it is at rest. Thus:

—Any object that occupies space equal to itself is either in motion or at rest. But since it cannot be in motion and at the same time occupy space equal to itself, it must be at rest.

—Every instant of time an arrow is in flight it occupies a space equal to itself and is therefore at rest. If it is at rest an infinite number of instants of time, then it is at rest the whole time.

Absolute Motion Cannot Even
Be Imagined

Absolute motion cannot even be imagined, much less known. Motion, as taking place apart from those limitations of space which we habitually associate with it, is totally unthinkable. For motion is changing of place; but in unlimited space change of place is inconceivable, because place itself is inconceivable. Place can be conceived only by reference to other places; and in absence of other places dispersed through space, a place could be conceived only in relation to the limits of space; whence it follows that in unlimited space place cannot be conceived—all places must be equidistant from boundaries that do not exist. Thus while we are obliged to think that there is an absolute motion, we find absolute motion incomprehensible.

—HERBERT SPENCER

Plutarch said that Homer, the great poet of antiquity, died of exasperation because he could not solve the riddle posed by a fisherman: "What we have caught we threw away; what we could not catch we kept." Someone should have told Homer that the answer is *fleas*.

Paradox of the Monday Drunkards

Somebody has told me of a dealer in gin who, having had his attention roused to the enormous waste of liquor caused by the unsteady hands of drunkards, invented a counter which through a simple act of contrivances gathered into a common reservoir all the spillings that previously had run to waste. St. Monday, as it was then called in English manufacturing towns, formed the jubilee day in each week for the drunkards; and it was now ascertained (i.e., subsequently to the epoch of the artificial counter) that oftentimes the mere "spilth" of St. Monday supplied the entire demand of Tuesday. It struck me, therefore, on reviewing this case, that the more they drank the more they would *titubate,* by which word it was that I expressed the reeling and stumbling of intoxication. If they drank abominably, then of course they would titubate abominably; and titubating abominably, inevitably they would spill in the same ratio.

The more they drank, the more they would titubate; the more they titubated, the more they would spill; and the more they spilt, the more, it is clear, they did *not* drink. You can't tax a man with drinking what he spills. It is evident, from Euclid, that the more they spilt, the less they could have to drink. So that, if their titubation was excessive, then their spilling must have been excessive, and in that case they must have practiced almost total abstinence. Spilling nearly all, how could they have left themselves anything worth speaking of to drink? Yet again, if they drank nothing worth speaking of, how could they titubate? Clearly they could not, and not titubating, they could have no reason for spilling, in which case they must have drunk the whole—that is, they must have drunk to the whole excess imputed, which doing, they were dead drunk, and must have titubated to extremity, which doing, they must have spilt nearly the whole. Spilling the whole they could not have been drunk. Ergo, they could not have titubated. Ergo, could not have spilt. Ergo, must have drunk the whole. Ergo, were dead drunk. Ergo, must have titubated. And so round again, in *secula seculorum.*

—THOMAS DE QUINCEY

Space

Will the gentle reader be so kind as to join me in con-
templating, for a few minutes, the Infinite Space which
surrounds our tiny planet. We believe—those of us,
at least, who answer fully to that ancient definition
of Man, "animale rationale"—that it is infinite. And
that, not because we profess to have grasped the conception of Infinity, but because the contrary hypothesis
contradicts Reason—and what contradicts Reason we
feel ourselves authorized to deny. Both conceptions—
that Space has a limit, and that it has none—are *beyond* our Reason: but the former is also *against* our
Reason, for we may fairly say "When we have reached
the limit, what then? What do we come to? There
must be either Something, or Nothing. If Something,
it is *full* Space, 'plenum'; if Nothing, it is *empty* Space,
'vacuum.' That there should be neither of these is
absurd. Such an hypothesis is intolerable."

—LEWIS CARROLL

"There ain't no sky," said one little boy to another.

"Well," replied the second little boy, "then tell me what is it that ain't?"

The Infinite Hotel

In the world of infinity a part may be equal to the whole! This is probably best illustrated by an example taken from one of the stories about the famous German mathematician David Hilbert. They say that in his lectures on infinity he put this paradoxical property of infinite numbers in the following words:

"Let us imagine a hotel with a finite number of rooms, and assume that all the rooms are occupied. A new guest arrives and asks for a room. 'Sorry,' says the proprietor, 'but all the rooms are occupied.' Now let us imagine a hotel with an *infinite* number of rooms, and all the rooms are occupied. To this hotel, too, comes a new guest and asks for a room.

" 'But of course!' exclaims the proprietor, and he moves the person previously occupying room N1 into N2, the person from room N2 into N3, the person from N3 into room N4, and so on. . . . And the new customer receives room N1, which became free as the result of these transpositions.

"Let us imagine now a hotel with an infinite number of rooms, all taken up, and an infinite number of new guests who come in and ask for rooms.

" 'Certainly, gentlemen,' says the proprietor, 'just wait a minute.'

"He moves the occupant of N1 into N2, the occupant of N2 into N4, the occupant of N3 into N6, and so on, and so on. . . .

"Now all the odd-numbered rooms become free and the infinity of new guests can easily be accommodated in them."

—GEORGE GAMOW

The Stocking Puzzle

If a stocking has been darned so much that not a thread of the original fabric remains, is it the same stocking?

Years ago this perplexed many scholars. Francis Bowen in his *Treatise on Logic* solves it thus:

"The answer lies in the fact that *sameness* or *identity* is an absolute term, which can neither be affirmed nor denied except in an unqualified sense, and that all which can be truly predicted of what comes short of *sameness* is *similarity*."

Geographical Question

If the Northern Hemisphere were land, and all the Southern Hemisphere water, ought we call the Northern Hemisphere an island, or the Southern Hemisphere a lake?

—AUGUSTUS DE MORGAN

Touch and Sight

Suppose a man born blind, and now adult, and taught by his touch to distinguish between a cube and a sphere (suppose) of ivory, of the same bigness, so as to tell when he felt one and t'other, which is the cube, which the sphere. Suppose then, the cube and the sphere [be] placed on a table, and the blind man be made to see; query whether by his sight, before he touch'd them, he could now distinguish and tell which is the globe, and which the cube. I answer not; for tho' he has obtained the experience of how a globe, how a cube affects his touch, yet he has not yet attained the experience that what affects my touch so or so must affect sight so or so; or that a protuberant angle in the cube that press'd his hand unequally shall appear to his eye as it does in the cube.

—WILLIAM MOLYNEUX

The Man Who Climbed the Mountain

Arthur Koestler, and others before him, relates that at sunrise one day an adventurous fellow set out to visit some friends encamped at the summit of a mountain. He struggled up a narrow path on the side of the mountain, walking at varying speeds, stopping sometimes to enjoy the view, to rest, and to eat food that he carried. At sunset he reached his destination at the top.

The man remained with his friends several days, then set out at sunrise for the trip down the mountain, over the same narrow path he used on the upward trip. But his speed on the descent was somewhat greater than it was on the ascent.

Problem: Prove that on the descent this man reached a place on the path that *at the same time of day* he had occupied on his way up—and that it was not coincidence.

Solution: Obviously, the descending man is going to reach a spot on the trail that he had passed on his way up.

Less obvious but equally true, wherever the place on the path may be, it will be passed by the descender at the same time of day it was passed by the ascender. In other words, if both trips were begun at sunrise, the descender cannot avoid passing the same spot at the same time as he did on the way up. No matter where the descending man figuratively meets himself on the way up, it will have to be at exactly the same time as the ascent.

Stated another way, it is the same as if two different men trod the same path on the same day—one ascending, the other descending. They will meet, occupy the same place on the path, and it will be the same time of day for both of them.

The Liar

This famous Sophism is said to have puzzled even Aristotle. Diogenes Laertes reported that Chrysippus the Stoic wrote six different treatises on it, and that Philetas, the grammarian and poet of Cos, studied himself to death in a vain effort to solve it:

Epimenides says that all Cretans are liars. But Epimenides himself is a Cretan; therefore he is a liar. But if he is a liar, then his statement is a lie and the Cretans are veracious. If the Cretans, including Epimenides, are veracious, then Epimenides is telling the truth when he says all Cretans are liars. But the difficulty is that he, as one among the Cretans, has by implication called himself a liar; therefore he is not telling the truth when he says all Cretans are liars.

The same problem may be stated in briefer form thus: If you say you lie, and say so truly, then you do lie; but if you say so falsely, then you speak the truth. In either case the same assertion is both true and false.

P. E. B. Jourdain, devised a variation of the above when he proposed that a card have on the front of it only the words "On the other side of this card is written a true statement." Turning the card over one would find written only the following: "On the other side of this card is written a false statement."

Incidentally, it is interesting to note that St. Paul said "One of themselves, *even* a prophet of their own, said, The Cretans are always liars, beasts, slow bellies. This witness is true."

—TITUS, 1.12, 13.

There is no impossibility in supposing that the man habitually lies, but that in this particular case (that is, in the admission of his own untruthfulness) he is telling the truth.

—ARISTOTLE

Can we describe as mendacious an utterance which is so designed by the utterer himself?

—GOMPERZ

A great philosopher pronounces the people of Crete, one and all, liars. But this great philosopher, whose name is Epimenides, happens himself to be a Cretan. On his own showing, therefore, Epimenides is a liar. But if so, what he says is a lie. Now what he says is that the Cretans are liars. This, therefore, as coming from a liar, is a lie; and the Cretans, as is now philosophically demonstrated, are all persons of honor and veracity. Consequently, Epimenides is such. You may depend on everything he says. But what he says most frequently is that all the Cretans are liars. Himself, therefore, as one amongst them, he denounces as a liar. Being such, he has falsely taxed the Cretans with falsehood, and himself amongst them. It is false, therefore, that Epimenides is a liar. Consequently, in calling himself by implication a liar, as one amongst the Cretans, he lied. And the proof of his veracity rests on his having lied. And so on *da capo* for ever and ever.

—THOMAS DE QUINCEY

Find the Liar

For the present purpose you must assume that all Indians are liars and that all white men are truthful.

A man was walking down a lonely country road at dusk and indistinctly saw three men approaching him. He halted and called out apprehensively, "Are you Indians or white men?"

One of the three men replied, but not loud enough to be heard by the questioner. Another of the three men called out, "He said he is white, and he is white, and so am I." The third man called out, "He is an Indian, but I am white."

How many were Indians and how many white?

Since, for the sake of the story, all Indians are liars, they would naturally say they were white; and the whites, being unfailingly truthful, would say they were white.

Therefore, the first man must have said "I am white".

The second man told the truth when he quoted the first man as saying he was white. Therefore the second man must have been white. Moreover, the second man verified that the first man was actually white, and it must have been so because the second man could not lie, since he was white.

Since the first two men are unquestionably white, the third man must be an Indian because he lied when he said that the second man was an Indian.

The Clever Missionary

A missionary is shipwrecked on an island where there are two tribes of natives—the liars and the truthtellers. The liars always lie when they speak, and the other tribe always tells the truth. The missionary wishes to go to the town of A, but as he goes, he comes to a fork in the road. He sees a native standing there bu doesn't know to which tribe the native belongs. What one question can the missionary ask to find out which road to take, regardless of which tribe the native belongs to? The answer is that the missionary asks, "Which road would another member of your tribe tell me to take if I wanted to get to the town of A?"

If the native were a truthteller, he would tell the truth. And if he were a liar, he would lie about what a liar would say, and thus he, too, would tell the truth. The missionary finds out which road to take, but he doesn't know whether the native was a liar or not.

The same missionary on the same island comes to a multiple intersection of roads. He sees the same native (of unknown honesty). What *one* question can he ask the native to find which road to take and whether the native is a truthteller or not?

The missionary asks, "Which of all these roads does *not* lead to the town of A?" The liar will point to the one road that does lead to A, and the truthteller will point to all the other roads except the one that *does* go there. In either case, the single road to take is clearly indicated, and the multiplicity of the answer is inversely proportional to the honesty of the native! One might think that information theory would forbid getting so much information from a single question. But the fact that the question does not have a simple yes or no answer makes the analysis more complex than first meets the eye.

—M. H. Greenblatt

When one finds a dilemma rushing at him, one can do what Baron Munchausen did when he found an angry wolf rushing at him. Unarmed, Munchausen waited until the raging beast was on top of him; then he reached his hand into the animal's mouth, down into the gullet, and on through the stomach until he got hold of the wolf's tail; then he simply turned the wolf inside out and sent him off in the opposite direction.

Mysterious Message

One day a young man was stopped on the street by a total stranger and was handed a note with the remark "Here is a message for you." The young fellow looked at the note but could not read it; it was in a strange and cryptic language. He showed the note to his girl friend, a young lady of scholarly attainments. She looked at it and promptly slapped the young man's face. Deeply disturbed, the youth took the note to the head of the languages department of the college he attended. This eminent personage glanced at the slip of paper and immediately ordered that the lad be expelled from the school.

Finally the young man heard of a venerable scholar, living in hermit-like retirement, who could translate just about anything and who surely would tell the truth about the content of the note. So the youth trudged miles and miles through the wilderness to the remote cabin of the scholar. The old man listened sympathetically to the youth's story and agreed to translate it and tell him exactly what it said.

The young man reached excitedly into his pocket for the note—but it was not there. He had lost it.

Sancho Panza Solves A Paradox

A stranger put the following case to Sancho Panza:

A large river divided a country. A bridge crosses this river. At one end of the bridge stands a gallows and a court of four judges for the execution of the following law:

"Whoever intends to cross this bridge must first declare under oath whither he goes, and what his business is. If he swears to the truth, he may go on; but if he swears falsely, he shall be hanged and die upon the gibbet at the end of the bridge."

One day a stranger came to the bridge and swore before the judges that he had come to die upon the gallows, and for no other reason. This puzzled the judges. They reasoned that if they let the man pass he had sworn falsely, and therefore under the law ought to die. But if they hang him he has sworn the truth, and then by the same law they should let him pass.

"Now your Lordship's judgment," they said to Sancho Panza," is desired as to what the judges ought to do with this man?"

"The question may be answered thus," said Sancho Panza. "There is as much reason to put this man to death as to let him live and pass the bridge; for if Truth saves him, the Lie condemns him. Since there's as much reason to bring him off as to condemn him, they should let him go free; for 'tis always more commendable to do Good than Hurt. When the scale of Justice is even, or a case is doubtful, we should prefer Mercy before Rigor."

—Abridged from CERVANTES' *Don Quixote*

Hempel's Paradox

Suppose we wish to investigate the truth of the statement that all red-headed secretaries at a particular company are married, and assume, further, that this investigation is to be done at a place where there are one thousand secretaries, three hundred of whom have red hair, and one hundred of whom are not married. We can assign the class of red-haired secretaries to A and the class of married secretaries to B. To investigate the statement that all red-haired secretaries are married, we would have to ask three hundred red-headed secretaries if they *were married*—three hundred questions. On the other hand, if we were to investigate the equivalent statement "All not-married secretaries are not red-haired," then we have only one hundred people to question. It is obviously more economical to use the inverted form of the logical statement. . . . This seeming inconsistency is known as Hempel's Paradox.

—M. H. GREENBLATT

Relative Problems

A man who committed suicide left behind this note:

"I married a widow. She had a grown daughter. My father married this stepdaughter of mine, and thus he became my son-in-law, and my stepdaughter became my mother when she married my father.

"My wife then gave birth to a son. This son was my father's brother-in-law, but he was also my uncle since he was the brother of my stepmother (who was also my stepdaughter).

"My father's wife also gave birth to a son. This son was both my brother and my grandchild—he was my father's child and my stepdaughter's child.

"Now, since this son of my father and of my stepdaughter is my brother, then my wife is my grandmother! If a grandmother's husband is a grandfather, then I am my own grandfather."

—HERBERT V. PROCHNOW

The Governor of Kgovjni wants to give a very small dinner party, and invites his father's brother-in-law, his brother's father-in-law, his father-in-law's brother, and his brother-in-law's father.

The Governor, as a consequence, had only one guest.

—LEWIS CARROLL

A man asserted that two men who are not in any way related to one another can have the same sister. When he was challenged to prove this, he drew up the following chart:

Miss Brown married Mr. Smith.   Mrs. Jones married Mr. Smith. They had a son, Harry.   They had a daughter, Susan.

Mrs. Jones married Mr. Johnson.
They had a son, George.

Harry Smith and George Johnson are not related.
But Susan Smith is the sister of both men.

People Are Still Arguing About This

A man stood looking at a portrait and said:

"Brothers and sisters I have none,
But that man's father is my father's son."

Most people stoutly assert that the speaker was referring to a portrait of himself. Another faction insists that a father (and only child) is looking at a portrait of his own son.

Epitaph

Ye mortals, as you're passing by,
Remark that near this monument doth lie,
    Centered in dust,
Two husbands, two wives,
Two sisters, two brothers,
Two fathers, a son,
    Two daughters, two mothers.
A grandfather, grandmother, and a granddaughter,
An uncle, an aunt, and their nieces followed after.
This catalogue of persons mentioned here
Was only *five*, and all from incest clear.

Epitaph

Here Lyeth the Body of Christ Burraway,
who departeth the Life Ye 18 days of October,
Anno Domini 1730. Aged 59 years.
  And there Lyes
ALICE who by his Life
Was my Sister, my mistress,
My mother and my wife.
Dyed Feb. Ye 12, 1729.
Aged 76 years.

The explanation of this peculiar epitaph is found in the fact that in 1670 a farmer at Martham named Christ Burraway seduced his twenty-seven-year-old daughter, Alice. She bore him a son who was sent secretly to a foundling home some distance away. When the son was twenty he was apprenticed to a farmer. Some time later he wandered through the country, came to Martham and applied to Alice Burraway for a job. His sister-mother unaware of his identity, employed him. The father was dead. Alice Burraway became fond of him and became his mistress. Later they were married and lived as man and wife for twenty years. When she was seventy-six years old Alice Burraway, noticing several moles on her husband's shoulder, suspected the truth, questioned him closely about his origin and early life, and realized she had married her son and brother.

Proving the Nonexistence of Death

The streets were almost deserted. A steeple clock struck two. It was good, he reflected, that he did not have to keep office hours, and that he could sleep late tomorrow. He walked rapidly, surely, humming to himself. Finally he began to sing in a low rich voice that seemed strange to him. Perhaps, indeed, this is not I. Perhaps I am dreaming Perhaps this is my last dream, the deathbed dream! He remembered an idea that Leinbach once, years ago, had expounded to a large gathering quite seriously, in fact with a certain impressiveness. Leinbach had discovered a proof that there really is no death. It is beyond question, he had declared, that not only at the moment of drowning, but at all the moments of death of any nature, one lives over again his whole past life with a rapidity inconceivable to others. This remembered life must also have a last moment, and this last moment its own last moment, and so on, and hence, dying is itself eternity, and hence, in accordance with the theory of limits, one may approach death but can never reach it.

—ARTHUR SCHNITZLER, *Flight Into Darkness*

How to Defeat Death

There was once a man who said to himself, "When I travel from the Atlantic to the Pacific on a railroad train, I gain three hours. When I go all the way around the world I gain a day. Now supposing I travel all the time! I'd never die, because I would never be quite as many days old as I would have been had I not kept moving."

"Daddy, can God do everything?"

"Yes, son, He can."

"Well, then, can God make a stone so big he could not move it?"

The record does not reveal the father's answer, but it could have been that God cannot do a thing that would destroy His own omnipotence.

The Problem of Evil

The Gods can either take away evil from the world
and will not, or being willing to do so cannot; or they
neither can nor will, or lastly, they are both able and
willing. If they have the will to remove evil and cannot, they are not omnipotent. If they can but will not,
then they are not benevolent. If they are neither able
nor willing, they are neither omnipotent or benevolent.
Lastly, if they are both able and willing to annihilate
evil, how does it exist?

—EPICURUS

To refute the idea that a rope of sand is worthless, Augustus De Morgan suggests that the sand can be made into glass, the glass spun into thread, and then a rope made of the thread.

Tristram Shandy's Dilemma

I am this month one whole year older than I was this time twelve-month; and having got, as you perceive, almost into the middle of my fourth volume—and no farther than to my first day's life—'tis demonstrative that I have three hundred and sixty-four days more life to write just now, than when I first set out; so that instead of advancing, as a common writer, in my work with what I have been doing at it—on the contrary, I am just thrown so many volumes back—was every day of my life to be as busy a day as this—and why not?—and the transactions and opinions of it to take up as much description—and for what reason should they be cut short? as at this rate I should just live 364 times faster and I should write—It must follow, an' please your worships, that the more I write, the more I shall have to write—and consequently, the more your worships read, the more your worships will have to read.

—LAURENCE STERNE

... And One Solution

Tristram Shandy, as we know, employed two years in chronicling the first two days of his life, and lamented that, at this rate, material would accumulate faster than he could deal with it, so, that, as the years went by, he would be farther and farther from the end of his history. Now I maintain that, if he had lived for ever, and had not wearied of his task, then, even if his life had continued as eventfully as it began, no part of his biography would have remained unwritten. For consider: the hundredeth day will be described in the hundredth year, the thousandth in the thousandth year, and so on. Whatever day we may choose as so far on that he cannot hope to reach it, that day will be described in the corresponding year. Thus any day that may be mentioned will be written sooner or later, and therefore no part of the biography will remain permanently unwritten. This paradoxical but perfectly true proposition depends upon the fact that the number of days in all time is no greater than the number of years.

—BERTRAND RUSSELL

In a certain hamlet there is a single barber. This barber is smooth-shaven. He has an unvarying rule that he will shave all those, and only those, who do not shave themselves.

Who shaves the barber?

A startling statement, but stop a minute to consider it:

Tomorrow today will be yesterday and yesterday today was tomorrow.

—Mc. T. E. McTaggert

A *Mother and a Crocodile Debate*
The Possession of a Child

A crocodile seized an infant playing on the banks of a river, but promised to restore the child if the mother would tell him truly what would happen to it.

"You will never restore the child," cried the mother.

Replied the crocodile, "If you have spoken truly, I cannot restore the child without destroying the truth of your assertion. If you have spoken falsely, I cannot restore the child, because you have not fulfilled the agreement. Therefore, I cannot restore the child whether you have spoken true or falsely."

The mother said, "If you have spoken truly, you must restore the child by virtue of your agreement. If I have spoken falsely, that can only be when you have restored the child. Therefore, whether I have spoken truly or falsely, the child must be restored."

No doubt they continued to argue until someone with a club or gun came along to take care of the crocodile—or maybe the beast's hunger won out over argument.

Can I know what I don't know?

No, you cannot.

Well, there's a certain thing I don't know, and I know it. Then don't I know what I don't know?

I don't know.

Legal Dilemmas

Protagoras taught law to Euathlos on the condition that he would be paid in full for his services as soon as Euathlos won his first case.

But when Euathlos completed his legal studies he went into politics and never practiced law. He refused to pay Protagoras on the ground that he had never won his first case.

Protagoras sued Euathlos and argued as follows before the court:

"You will either win this case or you will lose it. If you win it, you will have won your first case and will be obliged to pay me. If you lose it, you must obey the court and pay me. Consequently, whether you win or lose the case, you must pay me."

Euathlos replied to the following effect:

"Granted, I will either win this case or I will not. If I win, the judgment of the court will be in my favor, and I will not have to pay you. If I lose, then I have not won my first case and do not have to pay you. Therefore, whether I win or lose, I need not pay you."

> One of two brothers killed a man in cold blood.
> But the brothers are Siamese twins.
> Can the State punish the bad brother without doing an injustice to the good brother?

W. W. Fearnside refers to Jack Kent's comic strip for March 6, 1957, King Aroo overhears one man reproving another for throwing away his future. At the time King Aroo has just learned that his own future is nothing but a smear of tea leaves, so he begins looking through ash cans for the future that got thrown away.

Are You Certain It Isn't All a Dream?

That our minds, souls, thinking powers (use what name we may) exist, is the thing of all others of which we are most certain, each for himself. Next to this, nothing can be more certain to us, each for himself, than that other things also exist; other minds, our own bodies, the whole world of matter. But between the character of these two certainties there is a vast difference. Any one who should deny his own existence would, if serious, be held beneath argument; he does not know the meaning of his words, or he is false or mad. But if the same man should deny that any things exist except himself, that is, if he should affirm the whole creation to be a dream of his own mind, he would be absolutely unanswerable. If I (who *know* he is wrong, for I am certain of my *own* existence) argue with him, and reduce him to silence, it is no more than might happen in his dream. It is not impossible that in a real dream of sleep, some one may have created an antagonist who beat him in an argument to prove that he was awake.

—Augustus De Morgan

If a man should pass through Paradise in a dream, and have a flower presented to him as a pledge that his soul had really been there, and if he found the flower in his hand when he awoke—Ay! and what then?

—SAMUEL TAYLOR COLERIDGE

The Concealed Deer

A man of the state of Cheng was one day gathering wood when he encountered and killed a deer, which he then concealed in a ditch and covered with leaves. In his joy he forgot where he hid the animal and on his way home he began to think he must have been dreaming.

Meanwhile a man who had overhead his words got the deer. When the man reached home he said to his wife: "A woodman dreamt he had got a deer, but did not know where it was. Now I have got the deer, so his dream was reality."

"It is you," replied the wife, "who have been dreaming. You saw the woodman. Did he get the deer? And is there really such a person? It is you who has the deer; and then can his dream be a reality?"

"It is true I have the deer," said the husband. "It is therefore of little importance whether the woodman dreamt the deer or if I dreamt the woodman."

When the woodman reached home he became annoyed at the loss of the deer. That night he dreamt where the deer was and who had it. In the morning he went to the place indicated by his dream and found the deer and took legal steps to recover it.

The magistrate delivered the following judgment: "The plaintiff began with a real deer and an alleged dream. He now comes forward with a real dream and an alleged deer. The defendant really got the deer which the plaintiff said he dreamt, and is now trying to keep it; while, according to his wife, both the woodman and the deer were but figments of a dream, so that no one got the deer at all.

"However, here is a deer, which you had better divide between you."

When the Prince of Cheng heard this story he cried out; "The magistrate himself must have dreamed the case."

—H. A. GILES, from the Chinese

A Dream Dilemma

Once upon a time. I, Chuang Tzŭ, dreamt I was a butterfly, fluttering hither and thither, to all intents and purposes a butterfly. I was conscious only of following my fancies as a butterfly, and I was unconscious of my individuality as a man. Suddenly I awoke, and there I lay, myself again. Now I do not know whether I was a man dreaming I was a butterfly, or whether I am now a butterfly dreaming I am a man.

Jeremy Taylor's Dream Dilemma

Jeremy Taylor was prettily and fastidiously troubled, who having used to put his trust in dearms, one night dreamed that all dreams were vain; for he considered, if so, then *this* was vain, and the dreams might be true for all this. (For who pronounced them *not* true except a vain dream?) But if *they* might be true then *this* dream might be so upon equal reason. And dreams *were* vain, because this dream, which told him so, was true; and so round again.

—THOMAS DE QUINCEY

The Dream Problem, Again

We do not see things in the same way when we are awake as we do in sleep; neither do we see them in the same way in sleep as when awake. Therefore, existence or nonexistence of things is not absolute, but relative to the sleeping or waking condition.

It is, therefore, probable that we see those things in sleep which in a waking condition do not exist. But they are not altogether nonexistent, for they exist in sleep. Those things which we see when we are awake, also exist, although they do not exist in sleep.

—SEXTUS EMPIRICUS

We Do Not See What We Think We See

You may say that you see your friend, Mr. Jones, walking along the street; but this is to go far beyond what you have any right to say. You see a succession of colored patches, traversing a stationary background. Those patches, by means of a Pavlov-conditioned reflex, bring into your mind the word "Jones," and so you say you see Jones; but other people, looking out of their windows from different angles, will see something different, owing to the laws of perspective; therefore, if they are all seeing Jones, there must be as many different Joneses as there are spectators, and if there is only one true Jones, the sight of him is not vouchsafed to anybody. If we assume for a moment the truth of the account which physics gives, we shall explain what you call "seeing Jones" in some such terms as the following. Little packets of light, called "light quanta," shoot out from the sun, and some of these reach a region where there are atoms of a certain kind, composing Jone's face, and hand, and clothes. These atoms do not themselves exist, but are merely a compendious way of alluding to possible occurrences. Some of the light quanta, when they reach Jones's atoms, upset their internal economy. This causes him to become sunburnt, and to manufacture vitamin D. Others are reflected, and of those that are reflected, some enter your eye. There they cause a complicated disturbance of the rods and cones, which, in turn, send a current along the optic nerve. When this current reaches the brain, it produces an event. The event which it produces is that which you call "seeing Jones." As is evident from this account, the connection of "seeing Jones" with Jones is a remote, roundabout, causal connection. Jones himself, meanwhile, remains wrapped in mystery. He may be thinking about his dinner, or about how his investments have gone to pieces, or about that umbrella he lost; these thoughts are Jones, but these are not what you see. To say that you see Jones is no more correct than it would be, if a ball bounced off a wall in your garden and hit you, to say that the wall had hit you. Indeed, the two cases are closely analogous.

We, do not, therefore, ever see what we think we see. . . .

Now you can verify the occurrences in yourself which you call "seeing Jones," but you cannot verify Jones himself. You may hear sounds which you call Jones speaking to you; you may feel sensations of touch which you call Jones bumping into you. If he has not lately had a bath, you may also have olfactory sensations of which you suppose him to be the source. . . . But if you regard these as affording evidence that he is there, you have missed the point of the argument. The point is that Jones is a convenient hypothesis by means of which certain of your own sensations can be collected into a bundle; but what really makes them belong together is not their common hypothetical origin, but certain resemblances and causal affinities which they have to each other. These remain, even if their common origin is mythical. When you see a man in the cinema, you know that he does not exist when he is on the stage, though you suppose that there was an original who did exist continuously. But why should you make this supposition? Why should not Jones be like the man you see at the cinema? He may get annoyed with you if you suggest such an idea, but he will be powerless to disprove it, since he cannot give you any experience of what he is doing when you do not experience him.   —BERTRAND RUSSELL

One of the elusive objectives sought by alchemists and other brave dreamers is the discovery or invention of a Universal Solvent. Perhaps they have been dissuaded from this pursuit because they had nothing which would hold the Universal Solvent when it was discovered.

An Arab chieftain needed a speedy horse for an important mission. He fixed upon two fine animals, owned by two brothers, and asked them to race for one mile to determine the winning horse to be surrendered to the chief. When his counselors argued that both brothers would simply ride their horses as slowly as possible in order to avoid winning and thus the surrender of the horse, the wily chieftain just smiled and said, "Oh, don't worry; they will be required to change horses before the race begins."

One For the Courts

Two business partners placed $20,000 in the hands of a lawyer as custodian, with an ironclad understanding that the lawyer was to make no withdrawals from the fund without the signature of both partners.

When one of the partners then went off on a vacation, the other partner went to the lawyer and told him that a note for $15,000 was due and had to be paid immediately out of the fund. The custodian asked for the two required signatures. The partner said the other man could not be reached, but that the note must be paid immediately to stave off bankruptcy. Reluctantly, the lawyer handed the partner $15,000 for the payment of the note, whereupon he disappeared completely.

When the other partner returned home he instituted suit against the custodian for the $15,000 paid out of the fund. The lawyer explained the circumstances, and when the partner still insisted upon payment, the lawyer said, "I paid out the money for the note not from the partnership fund, but rather from my own funds."

"Then give me the fifteen thousand that you did not draw out of the fund," said the partner.

"All right," said the lawyer, "but you must produce the two signatures."

Globe-Circling

Imagine we have a piece of string 25,000 miles long, just long enough to exactly encircle the globe at the equator. We take the string and fit it snugly around, over oceans, deserts, and jungles. Unfortunately, when we have completed our task we find that in manufacturing the string there has been a slight mistake, for it is just a yard too long.

To overcome the error, we decide to tie the ends together and to distribute this 36 inches evenly over the entire 25,000 miles. Naturally (we imagine) this will never be noticed. How far do you think that the string will stand off from the ground at each point, merely by virtue of the fact that it is 36 inches too long?

The correct answer seems incredible, for the string will stand 6 inches from the earth over the entire 25,000 miles.

To make this seem more sensible, you might ask yourself: in walking around the surface of the earth, how much further does your head travel than your feet?

—EDWARD KASNER AND JAMES R. NEWMAN

Going Round the Squirrel

Some years ago, being with a camping party in the mountains, I returned from a solitary ramble to find everyone engaged in a ferocious metaphysical dispute. The *corpus* of the dispute was a squirrel—a live squirrel supposed to be clinging to one side of a tree-trunk; while over against the tree's opposite side a human being was imagined to stand. This human witness tries to get sight of the squirrel by moving rapidly round the tree, but no matter how fast he goes, the squirrel goes as fast in the opposite direction, and always keeps the tree between himself and the man, so that never a glimpse of him is caught. The resultant metaphysical problem now is this: *Does the man go round the squirrel or not?* He goes round the tree, sure enough, and the squirrel is on the tree; but does he go round the squirrel? In the unlimited leisure of the wilderness, discussion had been worn threadbare. Everyone had taken sides, and was obstinate; and the numbers on both sides were even. Each side, when I appeared, therefore appealed to me to make it a majority. Mindful of the scholastic adage that whenever you meet a contradiction you must make a distinction, I immediately sought and found one, as follows: "Which part is right," I said, "depends on what you *practically* mean by 'going round' the squirrel. If you mean passing from the north of him to the east, then to the south, then to the west, and then to the north of him again, obviously the man does go round him, for he occupies these successive positions. But if, on the contrary, you mean being first in front of him, then on the right of him, then behind him, then on his left,

61

and finally in front again, it is quite as obvious that the man fails to go round him, for it is by the compensating movements the squirrel makes, he keeps his belly turned towards the man all the time, and his back turned away. Make the distinction, and there is no occasion for any further dispute. You are both right and both wrong according as you conceive the verb 'to go round' in one practical fashion or the other."

—WILLIAM JAMES

The Wisdom of Governor Sancho

After having traveled a great distance, Governor Sancho, with his attendants, came to a town that had about a thousand inhabitants. . . . The name of the place was the Island of Barataria. As soon as he was come to the gates, the magistrates came out to receive him. . . .

Next they carried him to the court of justice, where, when they had placed him in his seat . . . two old men appeared before him; one of them with a large cane in his hand, which he used as a staff.

"My lord," said the other, who had none, "some time ago, I lent this man ten gold crowns to do him a kindness, which money he was to repay me on demand. I did not ask him for it again for a good while, lest it should prove inconvenient. However, after perceiving that he took no care to pay me, I have asked him for my due; nay, I have been forced to dun him hard for it. But still, he did not only refuse to pay me again, but denied he owed me anything and said that 'if I lent him so much money, he certainly returned it.' Now because I have no witnesses of the loan, nor he of the pretended payment, I beseech your lordship to put him under his oath; and if he will swear he has paid me, I will freely forgive him before God and the world."

"What say you to this, old gentleman with the staff?" asked Sancho.

"Sir," answered the old man, "I owe he lent me the gold; and, since he requires my oath, beg you will be pleased to hold down your rod of justice, that I may swear upon it how I have honestly and truly returned him his money."

Thereupon the governor held down his rod, and in the meantime the defendant gave his cane to the plaintiff to hold, as if it hindered while he was to make a cross and swear over the judge's rod. This done, he declared it was true the other had lent him ten crowns, but that he had really returned him the same sum into his own hands. The great governor, hearing this, asked the creditor what he had to reply. He made answer that, since his adversary had sworn it, he was satisfied, for he believed him to be a better Christian than offer to forswear himself, and that perhaps he had forgotten he had been repaid. Then the defendant took his cane again and, having made a low obeisance to the judge, was immediately leaving the court; which, when Sancho perceived, reflecting on the passage of the cane and admiring the creditor's patience, after he had thought awhile, he suddenly ordered the old man with the staff to be called back.

"Honest man," said Sancho, "let me look at the cane a little; I have use for it."

"With all my heart, sir," answered the other, "here it is," and with that he gave it to him.

Sancho took it, and giving it to the other man, "There," he said." Go your ways, and Heaven be with you, for now you are paid."

"How so, my lord?" cried the old man. "Do you judge this cane to be worth ten gold crowns?"

"Certainly," said the governor, "or else I am the greatest dunce in the world. And now you shall see whether I have not a headpiece fit to govern the whole kingdom." This said, he ordered the cane to be broken in open court, which was no sooner done that out dropped the ten crowns. All the spectators were amazed, and began to look on their governor as a second Solomon.

—MIGUEL DE CERVANTES

If a cake is to be divided into halves and a quarrel develops as to which one is to do the cutting of it, each can be satisfied by having one person cut the cake and the other person have first choice for his piece of it.

The Fallacy of the One-Legged Stork

A servant who was roasting a stork for his master was prevailed upon by his sweetheart to cut off a leg for her to eat. When the bird came upon the table the master desired to know what was become of the other leg. The man answered that storks had never more than one leg. The master, very angry, determined to strike his servant dumb before he punished him, so took him the next day into the fields where they saw storks, standing on one leg, as storks do. The servant turned trimumphantly to his master, on which the latter shouted, and the birds put down their other legs and flew away.

"Ah, sir," said the servant, "you did not shout to the stork at dinner yesterday! If you had done so, he would have shown his other leg, too!"

—BOCCACCIO

The Present Moment

Let any one try, I will not say to arrest, but to notice or attend to, the *present* moment of time. One of the most baffling experiences occurs. Where is it, this present? It has melted in our grasp, fled ere we could touch it, gone in the instant of becoming. . . . It is only as entering into the living and moving organization of a much wider tract of time that the strict present is apprehended at all. It is, in fact, an altogether ideal abstraction, not only never realized in sense, but probably never even conceived by those unaccustomed to philosophic meditation. Reflection leads us to the conclusion that it *must* exist, but that it *does* exist can never be a fact of our immediate experience.

—WILLIAM JAMES

Crudely and popularly we divide the course of time into past, present and future; but, strictly speaking, there is no present; it is composed of past and future divided by an indivisible point or instant. That instant, or time-point, is the strict *present*. What we call, loosely, the present, is an empirical portion of the course of time, containing at least a minimum of consciousness, in which the instant of change is the present time-point.

—S. H. HODGSON

There is no such thing as the next moment. The interval between one moment and the next would have to be infinitesimal, since, if we take two moments with a finite interval between, there are always other moments in the interval. Thus if there are no infinitesimals, no two moments are quite consecutive, but there are always moments between any two.

—BERTRAND RUSSELL

The Two Clocks

Which is better, a clock that is right only once a year, or a clock that is right twice every day? "That latter," you reply, "unquestionably." Very good, now attend.

I have two clocks: one doesn't go *at all*, and the other loses a minute a day: which would you prefer? "The losing one," you answer, "without a doubt." Now observe: the one which loses a minute a day has to lose twelve hours, or seven hundred and twenty minutes before it is right again; consequently it is only right once in two years, whereas the other is evidently right as often as the time it points to comes around, which happens twice a day.

So you've contradicted yourself *once*.

"Ah, but," you say, "what's the use of it being right twice a day, if I can't tell when the time comes?"

Why, suppose the clock points to eight o'clock, don't contradict yourself again if you can help it.

You *might* go on to ask, "How am I to know when eight o'clock *does* come? My clock will not tell me." Be patient: you know that when eight o'clock comes your clock is right, very good; then your rule is: keep your eye fixed on your clock, and *the very moment it is right* it will be eight o'clock. "But—," you say. There, that'll do; the more you argue the farther you get from the point, so it will be as well to stop.

—Lewis Carroll

Diminishing Time By One-Half

"When you have walked forward on a moving train, from the rear car, toward the engine, did you ever think what you were really doing?"

"Why, yes, I have generally been going forward to the smoking car to have a cigar."

"Tut, tut—not that! I mean did it ever occur to you on such an occasion that absolutely you were moving faster than the train? The train passes the telegraph poles at the rate of thirty miles an hour, say. You walk towards the smoking car at the rate of thirty-four miles. Your absolute speed is the speed of the engine, plus the speed of your own locomotion. Do you follow me?"

I began to get an inkling of his meaning, and told him so.

"Very well. Let us advance a step. Your addition to the speed of the engine is trivial, and the space in which you can exercise it is limited. Now suppose two stations, A and B, two miles distant by the track. Imagine a train of platform cars, the last car resting at the station A. The train is a mile long, say. The engine is therefore within a mile of station B. Say the train can move a mile in ten minutes. The last car, having two miles to go, would reach B in twenty minutes, but the engine, a mile ahead, would get there in ten minutes. You jump on the last car, at A, in a prodigious hurry to reach Abscissa, who is at B. If you stay on the last car it will be twenty minutes before you see her. But the engine reaches B and the fair lady in ten minutes. You will be a stupid reasoner, and an indifferent lover, if you don't put out for the engine over these platform cars, as fast as your legs can carry you. You can run a mile, the length of the train, in ten minutes. Therefore you reach Abscissa when the engine does, or in ten minutes—ten minutes sooner than if you had lazily sat down upon the rear car, and talked politics with the brakeman. You have diminished time by one half. You have added your speed to that of the locomotive to some purpose."

—Edward Page Mitchell

Day Defined

The day is the same length of time as anything that is the same length as *it*.

—Lewis Carroll

Can the Past Be Changed?

In traditional and semi-mythical Buddhist thought, there is the idea of a perfected self, the Great Soul, the Buddha whose existence is outside Time. (This idea can be found elsewhere, in various esoteric traditions haunted by the notion of a self-created immortality, sometimes involving a body of finer and indestructible matter surviving death.) Now while this infinitely superior being can exist outside Time, in some blissful eternal Present, inspired by his compassion for ignorance and suffering he can also enter Time at will. He has been awarded, we might say, the freedom of the fourth dimension. And for him Time is reversible. That he can go into the past involves the idea that the past is still existing in its own time, and that brings us to the further and more bewildering idea that if these superior beings have such powers, it might be possible for them to begin changing the past.

—JOSEPH B. PRIESTLEY

Try to answer, or even seriously to ask the question, "Which is longer, past time or future time?" and you attempt the absurd. Try to state which is longer, the distance which you might travel through space to your right or that which you might go to your left, and how either of these compares with the distances which you might go in any one of the infinite number of other directions. You are involved at once in absurdity.

—RICHARD C. CABOT

The Man Who Meets His Younger-Self

Hans Reichenbach describes what might happen if we occupied a torus space and a man's world-line looped about itself:

"Some day you meet a man who claims that you are his earlier self. He can give you complete information about your present condition and might even tell you precisely what you are thinking. He also predicts your distant future, in which you will some day be in his position and meet your earlier self. Of course you would think the man insane and walk on. Your companion on world-line 1 (normal world-line) agrees with you. The stranger goes his way with a knowing smile; you lose sight of him as well as of your companion on world-line 1 and forget about both of them.

Years later you meet a younger man whom you suddenly recognize as your earlier self. You tell him verbatim what the older man had told you; he doesn't believe you and thinks you are insane. This time you are the one that leaves with a knowing smile. You also see your former companion again, exactly as old as he was when you last saw him. However, he denies any acquaintance with you and agrees with your younger self that you must be insane. After this encounter, however, you walk along with him. Your younger self disappears from sight and from then on you lead a normal life." [You have, of course, at the last got out of the loop in your world-line.]

75

Could the Earth Run Backward?

It has been pointed out that, if we can imagine observers moving away from the earth at speeds comparable to that of light, some curious time effects would appear. If they moved at exactly the speed of light, let us say, on Christmas Day, any earth light signals would remain the same so that they would, so to speak, stay in Christmas Day. But if they moved faster than the speed of light (a most unlikely event), the time would appear to be reversed for them, because they would overtake the signals sent out by Christmas Eve and then by the day before Christmas Eve, so that earth time would appear to be running backwards. Speeds faster than that of light can be imagined, but are not likely to be achieved, except in thought. But if thought moves, what is its speed?

—J. B. PRIESTLEY

Which reminds one of the old limerick:

There was young lady named Bright
Whose movements were faster than light;
    She went out one day
    In a relative way
And returned on the previous night.

The Reversibility of Time

If we can travel over the same road in an opposite direction, why could we not travel backward over the same "path of time"? But, in truth, as Whitehead and Russell stressed, we never travel over the same road again. When I travel to South Station in Boston in the afternoon, it is not the "same road" on which I traveled in an opposite direction in the morning; the road itself is a number of hours older!

—J. T. FRASER

Time-Order

If a light-signal is sent from the earth to the sun, and reflected back to earth, it will return to the earth about sixteen minutes after it was sent out. The events which happen on earth during those sixteen minutes are neither earlier nor later than the arrival of the light-signal at the sun. If we imagine observers moving in all possible ways with respect to the earth, and the sun, observing the events on the earth during those sixteen minutes to be earlier than the arrival of the light-signal at the sun, some will judge it to be simultaneous, and some will judge it to be later. All are equally right or equally wrong. From the impersonal standpoint of physics, the events on earth during those sixteen minutes are neither earlier nor later than the arrival of the light-signal at the sun, nor yet simultaneous with it. We cannot say that an event A in one piece of matter is definitely earlier than an event B in another unless light can travel from A to B, starting when the earlier event happens (according to A's time), and arriving before the later event happens (according to B's time). Otherwise the apparent time-order of the two events will vary according to the observer, and will therefore not represent any physical fact.

—BERTRAND RUSSELL

Lo! The Poor Foreman

Pietro Di Donato, author of the famous *Christ in Concrete*, loves to tell about the building foreman who remained after hours to look over a construction job and noticed a pile of bricks on the third floor that belonged on another floor. Since all the workers had gone for the day, the foreman decided to transfer the bricks himself. In the elevator shaft there was a barrel attached to a pulley. The foreman pulled this barrel up to the third floor, tied the rope at the ground level, climbed back upstairs to load the bricks into the barrel. When he had finished doing this, he returned to the ground and untied the rope, intending to lower the barrel slowly to the ground.

But the loaded barrel, which weighed a good deal more than the foreman, plunged down the shaft, while the foreman froze to the rope and ascended up the shaft as fast as the barrel went down.

When the barrel hit the ground the bottom of it fell out. This then made the foreman heavier than the barrel, and he landed down on the bricks while the barrel shot up the shaft.

The dazed foreman then let go of the rope, as a consequence of which the barrel dropped down on his head.

The Queen Introduces Alice
to a Fact of Modern Life

Alice never could quite make out, in thinking it over afterwards, how it was that they began; all she remembers is that they were running hand in hand, and the Queen went so fast that it was all she could do to keep up with her; and still the Queen kept crying, "Faster! Faster! Faster!" but Alice felt she *could not* go faster, though she had no breath left to say so.

The most curious part of the thing was, that the trees and other things round them never changed their places at all; however fast they went, they never seemed to pass anything. "I wonder if all the things move along with us?" thought poor puzzled Alice. And the Queen seemed to guess her thoughts, for she cried, "Faster! Don't try to talk!"

Not that Alice had any idea of doing *that*. She felt as if she would never be able to talk again, she was getting so much out of breath; and still the Queen cried "Faster! Faster!" and dragged her along.

"Are we nearly there?" Alice managed to pant out at last.

"Nearly there?" the Queen repeated. "Why we passed it ten minutes ago. Faster!" And they ran on for a time in silence, with the wind whistling in Alice's ears, and almost blowing her hair off her head, she fancied.

"Now! Now!" cried the Queen. "Faster! Faster!" And they went so fast that at last they seemed to skim through the air, hardly touching the ground with their feet, till suddenly, just as Alice was getting quite exhausted, they stopped, and she found herself sitting on the ground, breathless and giddy.

The Queen propped her up against a tree, and said kindly, "You may rest a little now."

Alice looked round her in great surprise. "Why, I do believe we've been under this tree the whole time! Everything's just as it was!"

"Of course it is," said the Queen; "What would you have it?"

"Well, in *our* country," said Alice, still panting a little, "you'd generally get to somewhere else—if you ran very fast for a long time, as we've been doing."

"A slow sort of country!" said the Queen. "Now here, you see, it takes all the running *you* can do, to keep in the same place. If you want to get somewhere else you must run at least twice as fast as that!"

—LEWIS CARROLL

Inference

Chuang Tzŭ and Hui Tzŭ had strolled to the bridge over the Hao, when the former observed, "See how the minnows are darting about! That is the pleasure of fishes."

"You not being yourself a fish," said Hui Tzŭ, "how can you possibly know in what the pleasure of fishes consists?"

"And you not being I," retorted Chuang Tzŭ, "how can you know that I do not know?"

"That I, not being you, do not know what you know," replied Hui Tzŭ, "is identical with my argument that you, not being a fish, cannot know in what the pleasure of fishes consists."

"Let us go back to your original question," said Chuang Tzŭ. "You ask me how I know in what consists the pleasure of fishes. Your very question shows that you knew that I knew. I knew it from my own feelings on this bridge."

—CHUANG TZŭ

Universe?

What sense is there in calling the universe a universe at all? How, that is, can the notion be *applied* at all? To call our world "the universe" is to imply that it is somehow to be conceived as a whole. But we could never actually treat it as such. For we could never know it well enough. It might be of such a kind as not to be a completed whole, and never to become one, either because it was not rigid, but unpredictably contained within itself inexhaustible possibilities of new developments, or because it was really a mere fragment, subject to incalculable influxes and influences from without, which, if reality were truly infinite, might never cease. But either of these possibilities would suffice entirely to invalidate reasonings based on the assumed identity of *our* world with *the* universe.

—F. C. S. SCHILLER

Are Parents Murderers?

Jones was a congenital genius, and we always expected he would come to a bad end, poor fellow. Hence I was not surprised to find that after an early marriage and a brief but brilliant matrimonial career (including two pairs of twins and a triplet), he should have taken up his residence in an asylum which shall be nameless, but where I occasionally visit him. . . . The last time I saw him he startled me with a fallacy which seemed to me not unworthy of mention by the side of the *Liar* and the *Crocodile*.

Jones had been greatly depressed; he declared himself a murderer, and would not be comforted. Suddenly he asked me a question. "Are not the parents the cause of the birth of their children?" said he. "I suppose so," said I. "Are not all men mortal?" "That also may be admitted." "Then are not the parents the cause of the death of their children, since they know they are mortal? And am not I a murderer?" I was, I own, puzzled. At least I thought of something soothing. I pointed out to Jones that to cause the death of another was not necessarily murder. It might be manslaughter or justifiable homicide. "Of which of these am I guilty?" he queried. I could not say because I had never seen the Jones family, but I hear Jones has become a very great bore in the asylum by his unceasing appeals to everyone to tell him whether he has committed murder, manslaughter, or justifiable homicide!

—F. C. S. Schiller

Who Drinks Water? Who Owns the Zebra?

1. There are five houses, each of a different color and inhabited by men of different nationalities, with different pets, drinks, and cigarettes.
2. The Englishman lives in the red house.
3. The Spaniard owns the dog.
4. Coffee is drunk in the green house.
5. The Ukrainian drinks tea.
6. The green house is immediately to the right (*your* right) of the ivory house.
7. The Old Gold smoker owns snails.
8. Kools are smoked in the yellow house.
9. Milk is drunk in the middle house.
10. The Norwegian lives in the first house on the left.
11. The man who smokes Chesterfields lives in the house next to the man with the fox.
12. Kools are smoked in the house next to the house where the horse is kept.
13. The Lucky Strike smoker drinks orange juice.
14. The Japanese smokes Parliaments.
15. The Norwegian lives next to the blue house.

Now, who drinks water? And who owns the zebra?

Deduce, analyze, and persist. Then—and only then—turn to the next page for the answers.

ANSWERS: The Norwegian drinks water. The Japanese owns the zebra.

HOUSES	Yellow	Blue	Red	Ivory	Green
INHABITANTS	Norwegian	Ukranian	Englishman	Spaniard	Japanese
PETS	Fox	Horse	Snails	Dog	Zebra
BEVERAGES	Water	Tea	Milk	Orange Juice	Coffee
CIGARETTES	Kool	Chesterfield	Old Gold	Lucky Strike	Parliament

—from *Life International*

II

Logic and Illogic

The Ten Boxes

During the past two decades scientists, mathematicians, logicians, and other brain-tormentors have been discussing The Paradox of the Ten Boxes. It goes like this:

Ten closed boxes are placed before you. They are labeled one to ten. You are told to open the boxes in their numbered sequence. You are reliably informed that one of these boxes contains an egg. This egg is "unexpected" or "surprising." That is, you cannot by argument deduce which box the egg is in; you would have to actually open the box containing it.

You look at the boxes and then begin to grapple with the problem. You conclude that the egg is not in the tenth box because, had you opened the boxes in sequence, and found the first nine boxes empty, there would be no unexpected element in finding the egg in the tenth box.

But, having mentally eliminated the possibility of the egg being in the tenth box, then there would be no surprise in finding it in the ninth box—and then in the eighth box, and seventh box, and so on to the first box. Each of these mental steps would remove the aspect of surprise from the next box to be opened.

In actuality, however, you begin by opening the first box, then the second, then the third, and you find the egg in the fourth box.

There is nothing wrong about either your argument before opening the boxes or your actions in opening them. But the conclusions are contradictory.

During a question period following a lecture, a man arose and put a foolish query to the speaker. The latter replied:

"The logic of your question makes me think of another. Can you tell me why fire engines are always red? You can't? Well, fire engines have four wheels and eight men. Four and eight are twelve. Twelve inches make a foot. A foot is a ruler. Queen Elizabeth was a ruler. The *Queen Elizabeth* is the largest ship that sails the seven seas. Seas have fish. Fish have fins. The Finns fight the Russians. The Russians are red. Fire engines are always rushin'. Therefore, fire engines are always red.

"I hope this answers your question also."

—FULTON OURSLER

Contradiction

"No rule holds true without some exceptions."
But this very remark is a rule.
Then it has exceptions.
Then there are rules without exceptions.

Logicians point out that the reasoning of the above is correct, the absurdity resulting from what is called the fallacy of *universal skepticism,* which involves a contradiction in terms—a belief that there can be no belief.

To illustrate how "correlation" can misguide the scientific method, Anthony Standen in his *Science Is a Sacred Cow,* writes:

"A man gets drunk on Monday on whiskey and soda; he gets drunk on Tuesday on brandy and soda water; and on Wednesday on gin and soda water. What caused his drunkenness? Obviously the common factor, the soda water."

Why Frenchmen Should Talk English

"Looky here, Jim; does a cat talk like we do?"

"No, a cat don't."

"Well, does a cow?"

"No, a cow don't, nuther."

"Does a cat talk like a cow, or a cow talk like a cat?"

"No, dey don't."

"It's natural and right for 'em to talk different from each other, ain't it?"

"Course."

"And ain't it natural and right for a cat and a cow to talk different from *us*?"

"Why, mos' sholy it is."

"Well, then, why ain't it natural and right for a *Frenchman* to talk different from *us*? You answer me that."

"Is a cat a man, Huck?"

"No."

"Well, den, dey ain't no sense in a cat talkin' like a man. Is a cow a man?—er is a cow a cat?"

"No, she ain't either of them."

"Well, den, she ain' got no business to talk like either one er the yuther of 'em. Is a Frenchman a man?"

"Yes."

"*Well*, den! Dad blame it, why doan' he *talk* like a man? You answer me *dat!*"

—MARK TWAIN

A Reply to Horne Tooke

When Horne Tooke said: "Men who have no rights cannot justly complain of any wrong," the following syllogistic reply was made: "Men who have no rights cannot justly complain of any wrong. We can justly complain. Therefore we are not men who have no rights."

Topping the Teacher

The Reverend Dr. Ritchie of Edinburgh, though apparently a clever man, once met his match when examining a student as to the classes he attended.

"I understand," said Ritchie, "that you attend all the classes for mathematics?"

"Yes, sir."

"How many sides has a circle?"

"Two."

"Indeed! What are they?"

"Inside and outside."

"And you attend the moral philosophy class, too?" pursued the doctor.

"Yes."

"Well, no doubt you have heard lectures on various subjects. Did you ever hear one on cause and effect?"

"Yes, sir."

"Does an effect ever go before cause?"

"Yes."

"Oh, really! Then give me an instance."

"A barrow wheeled by a man."

"How shall one catch the lions in the desert?" a tourist asked a wise old Arab.

"Well," replied the Arab, "consider that there is more sand than lions in the desert. The best way is to get a strainer, then strain out all the sand, and there are the lions!"

Why Themistocles' Child
Governed the World

The child of Themistocles governed his mother;
   The mother governed her husband;
   The husband governed Athens;
   Athens governed Greece;
   Greece governed the world;
   Therefore, Themistocles' child governed the world.

A Nervous Nellie warns people against being trapped into supporting Communists. For example, one should beware of supporting the United Nations, because Quakers support the U.N., and Quakers are Pacifists, and Pacifists are Socialists, and Socialists are the same as Communists.

Shouts the medicine man: "Don't take my word for it; don't take anybody's word for it; read what it says on the bottle and see for yourself."

Caught Again

Michael Ryan, of the Richmond, Virginia, Common Council, years ago had tricked the Mayor into losing a bet, whereupon the Mayor said he was not going to be caught again.

"Well," said Ryan, "if you are sure of winning this time, then you'll take me up. I'll give you a chance. I will bet you that I can prove, by your own admission, that you are on the other side of the river."

"I'll take that bet," said the Mayor.

Ryan then pointed to Manchester and asked if that was not one side of the river.

"Certainly," said the Mayor.

"And is not Richmond on the other side?"

"Yes," said the Mayor reluctantly and with a trace of suspicion.

"Are you not in Richmond," concluded Ryan, "and thus on the other side?"

The Mayor did not know what answer to give, so he bought the drinks.

"I swear I'll never make another bet," said the Mayor over drinks.

"I'll take you a dozen of porter on that," said Ryan.

"Done!" cried the Mayor excitedly.

And no sooner had he said it than he *was* done!

DUMB When you look around and see how people are
living today, it's not surprising they die young.
DUMBER Yes, but not everybody dies young. What
about all the old people you meet everywhere
you go?
DUMB I agree you still meet old people, but don't forget they belong to a former generation.

The Three Barbers

Jim and Joe decide to go to the barbershop for haircuts. There are three barbers in the shop: Carr, Allen, and Brown.

"I hope Carr is on the job," said Jim. "Brown is clumsy and Allen's hands shake since his illness."

"Oh, Carr is certain to be on the job," said Joe.

"Prove it!" challenged Jim.

"O. K.," said Joe. "Assume, for the sake of argument, that Carr is *out*. Now if Carr is out, and if Allen is also out, then Brown must be in the shop. Do you agree?"

"Yes, of course, since someone must be in the shop," said Jim.

"Now, then," resumed Joe, "with Carr out, and the hypothesis is that Allen is out, Brown is in. But, we know that as a result of Allen's illness he will never go out alone—Brown has always to be with him. Consequently, we must consider another hypothesis: *If Allen is out, Brown is out.* Do you agree?"

"I suppose so," replied Jim with a touch of reluctance.

"Then, if Carr is out," continued Joe, "we have to consider two hypotheses in force at the same time: 'If Allen is out, Brown is *in*,' and 'If Allen is out Brown is out.' But these two hypotheses are contradictory—they cannot both be true together!"

"Why not?" asked Jim.

"Well, if Carr is out, these two hypotheses are true together. But we know they cannot be true together; that would be absurd. Therefore Carr cannot be out."

"But," said Jim, "so long as Allen is *in*, I don't see why Carr cannot be out."

"You forget," replied Joe, "that we began by assuming that Carr is out. Then we recognized that Allen cannot be out and Brown in, and that when Allen is out Brown must also be out. Therefore Carr is in."

By this time they had reached the barbershop and found out who was in the shop.

—Adapted from LEWIS CARROLL

If it was so, it might be; and if it were so, it would be; but as it isn't, it ain't. That's logic.

—LEWIS CARROLL

Bruno observed that when the Other Professor lost himself, he should shout: "He'll be sure to hear himself, 'cause he couldn't be far off."

—LEWIS CARROLL

Why Study?

The more we study, the more we know.
The more we know, the more we forget.
The more we forget, the less we know.
The less we know, the less we forget.
The less we forget, the more we know.
So why study?

The Fallacy of Many Questions

The requirement of a Yes or No answer to the following questions leads to the absurd conclusion shown.

Is it not true that you must have lost that which you once had, but which you have no longer? Yes.

Did you not have ten counters when you commenced the game? Yes.

Have you ten counters now? No.

Then you have lost ten counters!

The one being questioned actually still had eight counters, having lost only two.

An Athenian Variation

He who has not lost a thing has it;
You have not lost horns;
Therefore, you have horns.

Why Worry

You have two chances: one of getting the germ, and one of not. If you get the germ, you have two chances: one of getting the disease, and one of not. If you get the disease, you have two chances: one of dying, and one of not. And if you die—well, you still have two chances!

—Evan Esar

If today is Thursday, then today is not not Thursday. This statement is true on Friday or any other day of the week as well as on Thursday.
—W. W. FEARNSIDE AND W. B. HOLTHER

Is one thing different from another?
Yes.
And is benefiting a person something different from the good?
Yes.
Then the good is not benefiting a person.

—DIOGENES LAERTES

In one of his plays Sacha Guitry relates that some thieves got into an argument over the division of seven pearls of great value. One of the men handed two of the pearls to the man on his right, then two pearls to the man on his left. "I will keep three pearls for myself" he said decisively.

Thereupon one of the other men said, "How come you keep three pearls for yourself?"

"Because I am the leader," was the crisp reply.

"The leader? How come you are the leader?"

"Because I have more pearls."

—W. W. FEARNSIDE AND W. B. HOLTHER

To illustrate the workings of logic, a professor asked his class, "Suppose two men came out of a chimney—one is clean, one dirty. Which takes a bath?"

"The dirty one, of course," replied a student.

"Bear in mind," said the professor, "that the clean man sees the dirty one and sees how dirty he is, and vice versa."

"Now I get it," said the student. "The clean one, seeing his dirty companion, concludes that he is also dirty—so he takes the bath. Is that correct?"

"No," said the professor. "Logic teaches us this: how could two men come out of a chimney, one clean and one dirty?"

Parental Common Sense

The old couple were eating their first meal with their son after his return from college.

"Tell us, John," said the father, "what have you learned in college?"

"Oh, lots of things," said the son, and he recited his various courses of study, and added, "I also studied Logic."

"Logic, what is that?" asked the father.

"It is the art of reasoning," replied the son. "Let me illustrate: How many chickens are on that dish?"

"Two," said the father.

"Well," said John, "I can prove there are three." Then he stuck his fork into one and said, "This is one, isn't it?" The father agreed. "And this is two?" said the youth, sticking his fork into the second chicken. "Yes," said the father.

"Well, then," concluded the son, "don't one and two equal three?"

"Well, I declare," exclaimed the old man. "You really have learned things at college. Well, Mother," continued the father, "I will give you one chicken, and I'll eat the other. And John, you can have the third chicken."

An eminent Logician who can make it clear to you
That black is white—when looked at from the proper
    point of view;
A marvelous Philologist who'll undertake to show
That "Yes" is but another and a neater form of "No."
                   —W. S. GILBERT

A professor lecturing on insects at a university, said: "I hold here in my hand a flea. Notice it is on my right hand. I order him to jump to my left hand. The flea obeys, as you can observe. Now I repeat the experiment, and again the flea obeys. Now notice that I remove the legs of the flea, and order it to jump again. But, as you can see, the flea does not jump.

"Therefore, we have scientific proof that a flea whose legs have been removed becomes deaf."

The Folly of Rationalization in Advance
of Personal Experience

I am standing on the threshold about to enter a room. It is a complicated business. In the first place I must shove against an atmosphere pressing with a force of fourteen pounds on every square inch of my body. I must make sure of landing on a plank traveling at twenty miles a second round the sun. I must do this while hanging from a round planet, head outward into space, and with a wind of ether blowing at no one knows how many miles a second through every interstice of my body. The plank has no solidity of substance. To step on it is like stepping on a swarm of flies. Shall I not slip through? Verily it is easier for a camel to pass through the eye of a needle than for a scientific man to pass through a door. And whether this door be a barn door or a church door, it would be wiser that he should consent to be an ordinary man and walk in rather than wait until all the difficulties involved in a scientific ingress are resolved.

—A. S. EDDINGTON

A man who insisted he was dead, in spite of the arguments and persuasions of his family and friends, was finally put into the hands of a psychiatrist. The doctor placed his patient in front of a mirror and told him to stand there for two hours and to keep repeating, "Dead men don't bleed."

After the two hours had passed, the psychiatrist took a needle, pricked the man's finger, pointed to the bleeding digit, and said, "There now. What does that prove?"

"It proves," replied the patient, "that dead men do bleed."

"Who did you pass on the road?" the King went on, holding out his hand to the Messenger for some hay.

"Nobody," said the Messenger.

"Quite right," said the King: "this young lady saw him too. So of course nobody walks slower than you."

"I do my best," the Messenger said in a sullen tone. "I'm sure nobody walks much faster than I do!"

"He can't do that," said the King, "or else he'd have been here first."

—Lewis Carroll

Three men—A, B and C—are blindfolded and told that either a red or a green hat will be placed on each of them. After this is done, the blindfolds are removed; the men are asked to raise a hand if they see a red hat, and to leave the room as soon as they are sure of the color of their own hat. All three hats happen to be red, so all three men raise a hand. Several minutes go by until C, who is more astute than the others, leaves the room. How did he deduce the color of his hat?

C asks himself: Can my hat be green? If so, then A will know immediately that he has a red hat for only a red hat on his head would cause B to lift his hand. A would therefore leave the room. B would reason the same way and also leave. Since neither has left, C deduces that his own hat must be red.

—Martin Gardner

The Ingenious Ignoramus

Into a small Russian village once came a rabbi to apply for the rabbinical post that was vacant there. He was a good and wise man, was the rabbi, but with all that a terrible preacher and a worse scholar.

On the Sabbath day, right after the morning service, he mounted the pulpit ready to deliver a sample sermon. But go ahead and speak when there is just nothing to say!

But how does the saying go? "Where there is Torah there is also *chocma.*"

"My masters," began the rabbi resolutely. "Do you know what *sedra* we read today and about what I'm going to preach to you?"

"No," answered the congregation with one voice.

"If you don't know, then you aren't worthy enough to have it explained to you!" cried the rabbi indignantly. And he left the pulpit.

Downcast with shame, the members of the congregation left the synagogue.

The following Sabbath morning the synagogue was again filled with worshipers, and once more the rabbi mounted the pulpit.

"My dear Jews," began the preacher, "do you know what *sedra* we read today and what passage of Torah I'm going to expound?"

Intimidated by its experience of the previous Sabbath, the congregation cried out like one man, "Yes, we know!"

"You do, do you? In that case, why do you need *me* to explain?" cried the rabbi impatiently. And he left the pulpit.

And the third Sabbath, when the congregation gathered again, the rabbi once more mounted the pulpit.

"My masters," he asked, "do you know what *sedra* we have this week and what it is that I'm going to preach about today?"

Now the members of the congregation were very canny and they had decided to profit from their past experience. So some cried out, "We know!" and some cried out, "We don't know!"

The rabbi was taken aback. For a moment he stood undecided. Then he sternly began to rebuke the congregation:

"For the life of me I can't see what you need me to explain it to you! My advice is: Let those of you who know tell those who don't know!"

And with these words he descended from the pulpit.

—Told by NATHAN AUSUBEL

Twin brothers on a Polar exploration trip were trapped at the North Pole by an earlier-than-expected freezeup. They were marooned, and each day for exercise and to keep warm they ran in circles around the Pole—running in opposite directions.

However, this ultimately created a problem, because each time one circled the Pole he lost or gained a day when he crossed the International Date Line. Consequently, since the two were running in opposite directions, when they finally returned to the United States one of the twins was wearing a long beard and carrying his baby brother in his arms.

Private Judgment

"Private Judgment," the right and the duty, is a thing unavoidable in any matter concerning which one takes an interest. For if a man resolves that he will implicitly receive, *e.g.* in religious points, all the decisions of a certain Pastor, Church, or Party, he *has*, in so doing, performed *one* act of private judgment, which includes all the rest.

—RICHARD WHATELY

A poor, emaciated fellow was brought before a beefy-faced, overfed judge. The prisoner was charged with stealing.

"So you were hungry," said the judge. "That is the reason you stole. Well, I'm hungry, too—every day. But I don't steal."

A man imprisoned for gambling was playing cards with his jailers. But when they caught him cheating they booted him out of the prison.

The Philadelphia car salesman said to the prospective buyer, "Why, if you get into this car at midnight you can be in Pittsburgh at four A.M."

The customer, indignant, said, "And what in hell would I do in Pittsburgh at four in the morning?"

Sophsitical Tricks

Does a person sitting stand, and is a sick man well?
Of course not.
You are wrong. He who rose from his seat stands, and
he who is healed is well. Sitting he rose, and a sick
man was made well; therefore, sitting he stands, and
a sick man is well.

This statue is a work of art, isn't it?
Yes.
It is yours?
Yes.
Therefore it is your work.

Do you know who is behind that door?
No.
The man behind that door is your father.
Therefore you do not know your father.

Is it possible for he who is silent to speak?
It is not.
But it is possible for Socrates to speak; but Socrates
is silent.
Therefore, it is possible for him who is silent to speak.

Why Self-Denial Is Not a Part
of the Good Life

He who has a confirmed habit of any kind of action exercises no self-denial in the practice of that action. A good man has a confirmed habit or virtue.

Therefore, he who exercises self-denial in the practice of virtue is not a good man.

Sillygisms

Dry Bread Better Than Wisdom and Virtue

Nothing is better than Wisdom and Virtue;
Dry Bread is better than Nothing;
Therefore, Dry Bread is better than Wisdom and Virtue.

To call you an animal is to speak the truth;
To call you an ass is to call you an animal;
Therefore to call you an ass is to speak the truth.

A Syllable Eats Cheese

A mouse eats cheese;
A mouse is one syllable;
Therefore, one syllable eats cheese.

The Fallacy of Figure of Speech

Whatever a man walks he tramples on;
A man walks the whole day;
Therefore, he tramples on the day.

The Fallacy of Ambiguous Words

All *criminal actions* ought to be punished by law;
Prosecutions for theft are *criminal actions;*
Therefore, prosecutions for theft ought to be punished
   by law.

Birds Are Beasts

Some animals are beasts;
Some animals are birds;
Therefore, birds are beasts.

Why 2 and 3 Are One Number

5 is one number;
2 and 3 are 5;
Therefore, 2 and 3 are one number.

Why Every Man is a Knave

He who calls you a man speaks the truth;
But he who calls you a knave calls you a man;
Therefore, he who calls you a knave speaks the truth.

Feathers Are Heavier Than Lead

Nothing is heavier than lead;
Feathers are heavier than nothing;
Therefore, feathers are heavier than lead.

126

Eggs Come From Eggs

Every hen comes from an egg;
Every egg comes from a hen;
Therefore, eggs come from eggs.

Why Some Beasts Are Not Animals

Some animals are not sagacious;
Some beasts are not sagacious;
Therefore, some beasts are not animals.

Expediency Becomes Justice

Every unjust act is inexpedient;
No unjust act is expedient;
No expedient act is unjust;
Therefore every expedient act is just.

Why Every Cat Has Three Tails

No cat has two tails;
Every cat has one tail more than no cat;
Therefore, every cat has three tails.

The Wicked Have the Most Good

Repentance is a good thing;
None have so much repentance as the wicked;
Therefore, none have so much good as the wicked.

Black Is White

White is a color;
Black is a color;
Therefore, black is white.

Why Feathers Are Contrary to Darkness

Light is contrary to darkness;
Feathers are light;
Therefore, feathers are contrary to darkness.

Why Dogs Are Horses

All horses are mammals;
All dogs are mammals;
Therefore, all dogs are horses.

5 Is Both Even and Odd

2 and 3 are even and odd;
2 and 3 are 5;
Therefore, 5 is both even and odd.

Every invalid needs medical care;
Every fallacy is invalid;
Therefore, every fallacy needs medical care.

Begging the Question

How do *you* know it?
Because *he* told me.
And how does *he* know it?
Because I told *him*.

One evening a professor of logic was out walking his dog. When in the course of his perambulation he passed the college library, his attention was directed to a man's call for help from one of the windows in the building.

"What's your trouble?" called out the kindly professor.

"I got locked in here by mistake," was the response. "Get the janitor to open the door and let me out."

The professor of logic stopped to think about it for a few seconds, then replied: "No man can be in the library after 6 P.M. You are a man. Therefore you are not in the library." Whereupon he resumed his walk.

Logic is neither a science nor an art, but a dodge.
—BENJAMIN JOWETT

III

Fun From
Philosophers

Proving that a Man's Dog Is His Father

You say you have a dog.

Yes, and a villain of a one, said Ctesippus.

And he has puppies?

Yes, and they are very like himself.

And the dog is the father of them?

Yes, he said. I certainly saw him and the mother of the puppies come together.

And is he not yours?

To be sure he is.

Then he is a father, and he is yours; ergo he is your father, and the puppies are your brothers.

Let me ask you one little question more, said Dionysodorus, quickly interposing in order that Ctesippus might not get in a word: You beat this dog?

Ctesippus said, laughing: Indeed I do; and I only wish that I could beat you instead of him.

Then you beat your father, Dionysodorus said.

—PLATO

Damning a Man when He Does
and when He Does Not

Euthydemus:—O Cleinias, are those who learn the
wise or the ignorant? . . .

Cleinias answered that those who learned were wise.

Euthydemus proceeded: There are those who you call
teachers, are there not?

The boy assented.

And they are the teachers of those who learn—the
grammar-master and the lyre-master used to teach
you and other boys; and you were the learners?

Yes.

And when you were learners you did not as yet know
the things which you were learning?

No, he said.

And were you wise then?

No indeed, he said.

But if you were not wise you were unlearned?

Certainly.

You then, learning what you did not know, were unlearned when you were learning?

The youth nodded assent.

Then the unlearned learn, and not the wise, Cleinias,
as you imagine.

At these words the followers of Euthydemus, of whom
I spoke, like a chorus at the bidding of their
director, laughed and cheered. Then, before the
youth had well time to recover, Dionysodorus took
him in hand, and said: Yes, Cleinias, and when
the grammar-master dictated to you, were they

the wise boys or the unlearned who learned the dictation?

The wise, replied Cleinias.

Then after all the wise are the learners and not the unlearned, and your last answer to Euthydemus was wrong.

—PLATO

The small but influential school of ancient philosophers called Cynics is by some said to have been so named from the Greek word for dog—a contemptuous allusion to the uncouth and aggressive manner adopted by many of those of the Cynic school.

False Opinion Has No Existence

SOCRATES   Can a man see something and yet see nothing?

THEATETUS   Impossible.

SOCRATES   But if he sees any one thing, he sees something that exists. Do you suppose that what is one is ever to be found among nonexisting things?

THEATETUS   I do not.

SOCRATES   He then who sees some one thing, sees something which is?

THEATETUS   Clearly.

SOCRATES   And he who hears anything, hears some one thing and hears that which is?

THEATETUS   Yes.

SOCRATES   And he who touches something, touches something which is one and therefore is?

THEATETUS   That again is true.

SOCRATES   And does not he who thinks, think some one thing?

THEATETUS   Certainly.

SOCRATES   And does not he who thinks some one thing, think something which is?

THEATETUS   I agree.

SOCRATES   Then he who thinks that which is not, thinks of nothing?

THEATETUS   Clearly.

SOCRATES   And he who thinks of nothing, does not think at all?

THEATETUS   Obviously.

SOCRATES   Then no one can think that which is not, either as a self-existent substance or as a predicate of something else?

THEATETUS   Clearly not.

SOCRATES   Then to think falsely is different from thinking that which is not?

THEATETUS   It would seem so.

SOCRATES   Then false opinion has no existence in us, either in the sphere of being or of knowledge?

THEATETUS   Certainly not.

When Morris R. Cohen was teaching philosophy at New York's City College a student interrupted one of his lectures and asked: "Professor Cohen, how do I know that I exist?"

Cohen looked at the questioner and replied: "And who is asking?"

If there is existence, there must be non-existence. And if there was a time when nothing existed, there must have been a time before that—when even nothing did not exist. Suddenly, when nothing came into existence, could one really say whether it belonged to the category of existence or non-existence?

—CHUANG-TZŬ

A round assertion of the nonexistence of anything which stands in the way is the refuge of a certain class of minds; but it succeeds only with things subjective; the objective offers resistance. A philosopher of the appropriative class tried it upon the constable who appropriated him: "I deny your existence," said he. "Come along all the same," said the unpsychological policeman.

—AUGUSTUS DE MORGAN

I thought I knew I knew it all,
But now I must confess,
The more I know I know,
I know I know the less.
—ANONYMOUS

Proving that To Desire One who Is Ignorant To Become Wise Is To Wish that One To Perish

Tell me, he said, Socrates and the rest of you who say that they want this young man [Cleinias] to become wise, are you in jest or in real earnest?

[Socrates replied that they were in dead earnest]

Reflect, Socrates; you may have to deny your words.

I have reflected, I said; and I shall never deny my words.

Well, said he, and so you say that you wish Cleinias to become wise?

Undoubtedly.

And he is not wise as yet?

At least his modesty will not allow him to say that he is.

You wish him, he said, to become wise and not be ignorant?

That we do.

You wish him to be what he is not, and no longer to be what he is.

I was thrown into consternation at this.

Taking advantage of my consternation he added: You wish him no longer to be what he is, which can only mean that you wish him to perish.

—PLATO

The Impossibility of Motion

If motion is possible, a body must move either in the place where it is, or in a place where it is not.

But a body cannot move in the place where it is; and of course, it cannot move where it is not.

Therefore, motion is impossible.

—DIODORUS THE MEGARIC

The above fallacy led to the famous phrase *Solvitur ambulando*—"It is solved by walking."

It is related that Herophilus, the Greek physician, was called to treat Diodorus for a dislocated shoulder and said to him: "Your shoulder has been put out either in the place where it was or where it was not; but it was neither where it was nor where it was not; therefore it has not been put out."

Diodorus no doubt replied: "Come now, stop the nonsense and fix the shoulder."

Zeno's Argument that Place Does Not Exist

"If everything that exists is somewhere," said Zeno, "and place exists, place also will be somewhere. And so place will be in a place, and so on *ad infinitum.*"

Zeno's argument seems to do away with place, putting the question as follows: if place exists, in what will it be? For every existent is in something; but what is in something is in a place. Place therefore will be in a place, and so on ad infinitum; therefore place does not exist.

—PHILOPONUS

Place Does Not Exist

The Peripatetics assert that place is "the limit of what encloses it so far as it encloses," so that my place is the surface of the air that forms a mould round my body. But if this is place, the same thing will both be and not be. For when the body is about to become in a certain place, then, inasmuch as nothing can become in what is nonexistent, the place must be preexistent in order that the body may in this way become in it, and consequently the place will exist before the-body-in-the-place becomes therein. But inasmuch as it consists in the moulding of the surface of what encloses round the thing enclosed, place cannot be already subsisting before the body becomes within it, and therefore it will not be in existence then. But it is absurd to say that the same thing both is and is not; therefore place is not "the limit of what encloses it so far as it encloses."

—SEXTUS EMPIRICUS

From the Chinese

Hui Tzŭ, an ancient Chinese philosopher, posed the two following problems:

If you take a stick a foot long and the first day cut it in half, and the second day cut the half in half, and then that half in half, and keep on doing the same, you will never come to the end of it.

A motherless colt never had a mother; for when it had a mother it was not motherless, and at every other moment of its life it had no mother.

A Chinese philosopher is supposed to have said that if there are a brown cow and a white horse, then there are three things, for the cow is one thing, the white horse another, and the two together a third thing.

Theological Question

Is not God the author of your reason?

Can He then be the author of anything which is contrary to your reason?

If reason be a sufficient guide, why should God give you any other?

If it be not a sufficient guide, why then has He given you *that*?

—ROBERT TAYLOR

The Fallacy of the Heap

Does one grain of wheat make a heap? If not one grain, then would two, or three? If three grains are a small number of grains, then may not the same be said of four, and if four then five, and so on to ten? But how can ten grains make a heap?

Another form of this fallacy is called the Bald-Head. When does a man have a bald head? A man who has lost a single hair surely can't be called bald. Neither can a man who has lost only two, three, or four hairs. And so on.

This fallacy agitated many of the ancient philosophers. The logician Chrysippus wrote a treatise on it. Cicero was stumped by it and reported that it was applied to such antitheses as rich and poor, famous and obscure, long and short, broad and narrow, and other pairs of opposites.

The fallacy's plausibility results from our tendency to allow language to deceive us into accepting degrees of differences for absolute differences.

Does a Single Grain of Grass Seed
Make a Noise In Falling?

"Tell me, Protagoras," said Zeno, "does a single grain of grass seed make a noise in falling, or the ten thousandth part of a grain?" And when Protagoras said it did not, Zeno asked, "Does a bushel of grass seed make a noise when it falls or not?" Protagorus replied that it did. Zeno then asked, "What then? Is there not a ratio of a bushel of grass seed to one grain of grass seed and the ten thousandth part of a grain?" Protagoras replied that there was. Zeno then asked, "Well, then, will not the ratio of the sounds to one another be the same?"

Aristotle Asserted that Zeno Was Wrong

Zeno's argument is not true, that there is no part of a grain of grass seed that does not make a sound; for there is no reason why any such part should not in any length of time fail to move the air that a whole bushel moves in falling.

Navel Battle

Hundreds of years ago theologians argued whether or not Adam and Eve had navels. Michelangelo and Raphael both pictured Adam with a navel. Other artists omitted navels or concealed the area with flowing locks. But Sir Thomas Browne was outspokenly anti-navel so far as Adam was concerned, remarking, "That tortuosity or complicated nodosity we usually call the 'Navell' is a dreadful mistake, notwithstanding the authentick draughts of Angelo and others." He argued that Adam with a navel implies that "the Creator affected superfluities or ordained parts without use."

Defenders of Adam's navel said that although superfluous in his case, the real purpose was to test man's faith—to determine whether one was reasonable or devout.

A Philosopher is a Fool who torments himself while he is alive, to be talked of after he is dead.

—JEAN D'ALBERT

The Do-Nothing Fallacy

If it is fated that you shall recover from the present disease, then you will recover whether you call in a physician or not. If it is fated that you shall not recover, then, with or without a physician, you will not recover.

But either the one or the other of these two contradictories is fated; therefore it will be no use to call in a physician.

Cicero, who stated the above fallacy, added that if this reasoning were correct, then our whole life would be reduced to a state of hopeless inactivity.

Zeno aptly refuted this same fallacy when he was whipping a slave. The slave called out, in excuse for his fault, that it was fated for him to steal. "And so it is fated for me to whip you," replied Zeno.

Medieval metaphysicians have been known to engage in discussions as to how many angels can dance on the head of a pin. When a student asked Wendell Johnson the same question, he replied: "Give me a pin and bring in some angels and I'll tell you!"

The Decline and Revival of Knowledge

"Which of your teachers do you value most highly, those whose words are easily understood, or those who puzzle you at every turn?"

I felt obliged to admit that we generally admired most the teachers we couldn't quite understand.

"Just so," said Mein Herr. "That's the way it begins. Well, *we* were at that stage some eighty years ago—or was it ninety? Our favorite teacher got more obscure every year; and every year we admired him more—just as *your* Art-fanciers call *mist* the fairest feature in a landscape, and admire a view with frantic delight when they can see nothing! Now I'll tell you how it ended. It was Moral Philosophy that our idol lectured on. Well, his pupils couldn't make head or tail of it, but they got it all by heart; and when Examination-time came, they wrote it down; and the Examiners said 'Beautiful! What depth!' "

"But what good was it to the young men *afterwards?*"

"Why, don't you see?" replied Mein Herr. "They became teachers in their turn, and *they* said all these things over again; and *their* pupils wrote it all down; and the Examiners accepted it; and nobody had the ghost of an idea what it all meant!"

"And how did it end?"

"It ended this way. We woke up one find day, and found there was no one in the place that knew *anything* about Moral Philosophy. So we abolished it, teachers, classes, Examiners, and all. And if any one wanted to learn anything about it, he had to make it out for himself; and after another twenty years or so there were several men that really knew something about it!"

—LEWIS CARROLL

Philosophical Puzzle

If a tree falls in a forest many hundreds of miles from any living creature, is any sound produced?

In other words, does the material world have an independent existence, or does it depend wholly upon our perception of it?

Andrei Bumblowski

Relates His Dream Experience in Hell

At the very center of the infernal kingdom is Satan, to whose presence only the more distinguished among the damned are admitted. The improbabilities become greater and greater as Satan is approached, and He Himself is the most complete improbability imaginable. He is pure Nothing, total non-existence, and yet continually changing.

I, because of my philosophical eminence, was early given audience with the Prince of Darkness. I had read of Satan as *der Geist der stets verneint,* the Spirit of Negation. But on entering the Presence I realized with a shock that Satan has a negative body as well as a negative mind. Satan's body is, in fact, a pure and complete vacuum, empty not only of particles of matter but also of particles of light. His prolonged emptiness is secured by a climax of improbability: whenever a particle approaches His outer surface, it happens by chance to collide with another particle which stops it from penetrating the empty region. The empty region, since no light ever penetrates it, is absolutely black— not more or less black, like the things to which we loosely ascribe this word, but utterly, completely and infinitely black. . . .

He is surrounded by a chorus of sycophantic philosophers who have substituted pandiabolism for pantheism. These men maintain that existence is only apparent; non-existence is the only true reality. They hope in time to make the non-existence of appearance appear, for in that moment what we now take to be existence will be seen to be in truth only an outlying portion of the diabolic essence. Although these metaphysicians showed much subtlety, I could not agree with them. I had been accustomed while on earth to oppose tyrannous authority and this habit remained with me in Hell. I began to argue with the metaphysical sycophants:

"What you say is absurd," I expostulated. "You proclaim that non-existence is the only reality. You pretend that this black hole which you worship exists. You are trying to persuade me that the non-existent exists. But this is a contradiction; and, however hot the flames of Hell may become, I will never so degrade my logical being as to accept a contradiction."

At this point the President of the sycophants took up the argument: "You go too fast, my friend," he said. "You deny that the non-existent exists? But what is this to which you deny existence? If the non-existent is nothing, any statement about it is nonsense. And so is your statement that it does not exist. I am afraid you have paid too little attention to the logical analysis of sentences, which ought to have been taught you when you were a boy. Do you not know that every sentence has a subject, and that, if a subject were nothing, the sentence would be nonsense? So, when you proclaim, with virtuous heat, that Satan—who is the non-existent—does not exist, you are plainly contradicting yourself."

"You," I replied, "have no doubt been here for some time and continue to embrace somewhat antiquated doctrines. You prate of sentences having subjects, but all that sort of talk is out of date. When I say that Satan, who is the non-existent, does not exist, I mention neither Satan nor the non-existent, but only the word 'Satan' and the word 'non-existent.' Your fallacies have revealed to me a great truth. The great truth is that the word 'not' is superfluous. Henceforth I will not use the word 'not.'"

At this the assembled metaphysicians burst into a shout of laughter. "Hark how the fellow contradicts himself," they said when the paroxysm of merriment had subsided. "Hark at his great commandment which is to avoid negation. He will NOT use the word 'not,' forsooth!"

Though I was nettled, I kept my temper. I had in my pocket a dictionary. I scratched out all the words expressing negation and said: "My speech shall be composed entirely of the words that remain in this dictionary. By the help of these words that remain, I shall be able to describe everything in the universe. My descriptions will be many, but they will all be of things other than Satan. Satan has reigned too long in this infernal realm. His shining armor was real and inspired terror, but underneath the armor there was only a bad linguistic habit. Avoid the word 'not,' and His empire is at an end."

Satan, as the argument proceeded, lashed His tail with ever-increasing fury, and savage rays of darkness shot from His cavernous eyes. But at the last, when I denounced Him as a bad linguistic habit, there was a vast explosion, the air rushed in from all sides, and the horrid shape vanished. The murky air of Hell, which had been due to inspissated rays of nothingness, cleared as if by magic.

—BERTRAND RUSSELL

Metaphysical Question

What is Mind?　*Answer:* No matter
What is Matter?　*Answer:* Never Mind
What is Soul?　*Answer:* It is Immaterial

The True Does Not Exist

He who says that something true exists either only asserts that something true exists or proves it. And if he merely asserts it, he will be told the opposite of his mere assertion, namely, that nothing is true. But if he proves that something is true, he proves it either by a true proof or by one that is not true. But he will not say that it is by one not true, for such a proof is not to be trusted. And if it is by a true proof, whence comes it that the proof which proves that something is true is itself true? If it is true of itself, it will be possible also to state as true of itself that truth does not exist; while if it is derived from proof, the question will again be asked: "How is it that this proof is true?" and so on ad infinitum. Since, then, in order to learn that there is something true, an infinite series must first be grasped, and it is not possible for an infinite series to be grasped, it is not possible to know for a surety that something true exists.

—SEXTUS EMPIRICUS

The Sophist is a speculator in sham wisdom.
—ARISTOTLE

Why Truth Is True

If a person says that "nothing is true," he may be replied to in this fashion:

You either believe this or you do not.

If you believe it, then you must maintain that it is true. That in turn means you deny that "nothing is true." If you do not believe that "nothing is true," then you deny that "nothing is true."

Therefore, whether you believe the statement or not, you reject the view that "nothing is true."

Socrates Was Not Born and Did Not Die

If Socrates was born, Socrates became either when Socrates existed not or when Socrates already existed; but if he shall be said to have become when he already existed, he will have become twice; and if when he did not exist, Socrates was both existent and non-existent at the same time—existent through having become, non-existent by hypothesis. And if Socrates died, he died either when he lived or when he died. Now he did not die when he lived, since he would have been both alive and dead; nor yet when he died, since he would have been dead twice. Therefore Socrates did not die.

—SEXTUS EMPIRICUS

Happiness Is Impossible

Every unhappy state occurs because of some perturbation. But every perturbation in men is a consequence due either to an eager pursuit of certain things or to an eager avoidance of certain things. And all men eagerly pursue what is believed by them to be good and avoid what is supposed to be evil. Therefore every case of unhappiness occurs owing to the pursuit of the good things as good, and the avoidance of the evil things as evil. Since, then, the Dogmatists firmly believe that this thing is good by nature and that thing is evil by nature, as he is always pursuing the one and avoiding the other and being, consequently, perturbed, he will never be happy. . . . Through continually pursuing what he believes to be good by nature and shunning what he supposes to be evil he will never be clear of perturbation, but both when he has failed as yet to grasp the good he will be extremely perturbed because of his desire to gain it, and when he has gained it he will never be at rest owing to the excess of his joy on account of keeping watch over his acquisition.

—SEXTUS EMPIRICUS

If you say there is a thing not-knowable, how do you know it?

—S. N. GUPTA

It cannot be denied that to affirm of the Ultimate Reality that it is unknowable is, in a remote way, to assert some knowledge of it, and therefore involves a contradiction.

—HERBERT SPENCER

Good Does Not Exist

If good exists, it ought to be desirable on its own account, since every man desires to obtain it even as he desires to escape evil. But, as we shall show, nothing is desirable on its own account; therefore there does not exist any good. For if there is anything desirable on its own account, either the desire itself is desirable or something other than this—for example, either the desire for wealth is desirable or wealth itself is desirable. But the desire itself will not be desirable. For if the desire is desirable on its own account, we ought not to be eager to obtain that which we desire lest we should cease from desiring any longer. For just as we ought to avoid drinking or eating lest by having eaten or drunk we should cease to wish any longer to drink or eat, so, if the desire for wealth or health is desirable, we ought not to pursue after wealth or health, lest by acquiring them we cease to desire them any longer. But we do desire the acquisition of them; therefore the desire is not desirable but rather to be avoided.

—SEXTUS EMPIRICUS

The Spanish Inquisition arrested Antonio Perez, minister of Philip II, because he threatened to cut off God's nose. The Holy Office was not so much disturbed by Perez's blasphemous threat, but rather because he held that God had a nose.

Contradiction! said Dionysodorus. Why, there never
was such a thing.

Certainly there is, replied Ctesippus. There can be no
question of that. Do you, Dionysodorus, maintain
there is not?

You will never prove to me, he said, that you have
heard anyone contradicting anyone else.

Indeed, he said, then now you may hear Ctesippus contradicting Dionysodorus.

Are you prepared to make that good?

Certainly, he said.

Well, then, are not words expressive of things?

Yes.

Of their existence or non-existence?

Of their existence. For, as you may remember, Ctes-
sippus, we just now proved that no man could
affirm a negative; for no one could affirm that
which is not.

And what does that signify, said Cleinias. You and I
may contradict for all that.

But can we contradict one another, said Dionysodorus,
when both of us are describing the same thing?
Then we must surely be speaking of the same
thing?

He admitted that.

Or when neither of us is speaking of the same thing?
For then neither of us says a word about the
thing at all?

He granted that also.

But when I describe something and you describe an-

other thing, or I say something and you say nothing, is there any contradiction? How can he who
speaks contradict him who speaks not?

—PLATO

Famous Question

What would happen if an irresistible force met an immovable object?

There is no solution to this because it is a contradiction in terms. If an irresistible force existed, then there could be no such thing as an immovable object. The two simply could not exist at the same time.

An elderly philosopher said, "If you will give me Aristotle's system of logic, I will force my enemy to a conclusion; give me the syllogism, and that is all I ask."

Another elderly philosopher said, "Just give me the Socratic system of interrogation, and I will run my adversary into a corner."

A third and much younger philosopher, who had listened to these remarks, said, "If you give me a little ready cash I will always gain my point. I will always drive my adversary to a conclusion—whatever conclusion I want him to reach—because ready cash is a wonderful clearer of the intellect."

No One Can Tell a Lie

Euthydemus replied: And do you think, Ctesippus, that it is possible to tell a lie?

Yes, said Ctesippus, I should be mad to say anything else.

And in telling a lie, do you tell the thing of which you speak or not?

You tell the thing of which you speak.

And he who tells, tells that thing which he tells, and no other?

Yes, said Ctesippus.

And that is a distinct thing apart from other things?

Certainly.

And he who says that thing says that which is?

Yes.

And he who says that which is says the truth. And therefore Dionysodorus, if he says that which is, says the truth and no lie.

Yes, Euthydemus, said Ctesippus, but in saying this, he says what is not.

Euthydemus answered: And that which is not is not?

True.

And that which is not is nowhere?

Nowhere.

And can anyone do anything about that which has no existence, or do to Cleinias that which is not and is nowhere?

I think not, said Ctesippus.

Well, but do rhetoricians, when they speak in the assembly, do nothing?

Nay, he said, they do something.

And doing is making?

Yes.

And speaking is doing and making?

He agreed.

Then no one says that which is not, for in saying what is not he would be doing something; and you have already acknowledged that no one can do what is not. And therefore, upon your own showing, no one says what is false; but if Dionysodorus says anything, he says what is true and what is.

—PLATO

Aristotle Suggests a Reply

An Athenian mother said to her son: "Do not enter into public business; for if you say what is just, men will hate you, and if you say what is unjust, the gods will hate you."

Aristotle suggests the son could well reply: "I ought to enter into public affairs; for if I say what is just, the gods will love me, and if I say what is unjust, men will love me."

Why God Is Not an Infinite Being

Whatever is real is limited by that which is not.
But whatever is limited is not infinite.
Therefore, if God is real, and not a mere fiction of the imagination, He is not an infinite being.

Why Nothing Becomes

Either the existent becomes or the non-existent.

Now the existent does not become (for it exists), nor yet does the non-existent (for the becoming is passive but non-existent is not passive).

Therefore, nothing becomes.

—ASCRIBED TO GORGIAS

Why the Greek Skeptics Refused to Accept an Argument They Could Not Refute

When someone proposes to us an argument that we cannot refute, we say to him: "Before the founder of the sect to which you belong was born, the argument which you propose in accordance with it had not appeared as a valid argument, but was dormant in nature, so in the same way it is possible that its refutation also exists in nature, but has not yet appeared to us, so that it is not at all necessary for us to agree with an argument that now seems to be strong."

—SEXTUS EMPIRICUS

Soul Proof

Matter is made up of molecules (size A) which are vortex rings composed of luminiferous ether. The ether is made up of much smaller molecules (size B), vortex rings in the subether. This is the Unseen Universe. Here the human Soul exists. It is made up of B molecules. It permeates the Body like a gas. Thought is vibratory motion in the A molecules, but part of the vibration, following the law of the conservation of energy, will be absorbed by the B molecules, the Soul. Therefore the Soul has memory. When the Body dies, the Soul keeps memory intact, and becomes a free agent in the subether. The physical possibility of the immortality of the Soul is thus demonstrated.

—BALFOUR STEWART AND PETER G. TAIT

Is Man a False God?

Since that is false which is accomodated to the likeness of something and, nevertheless, is not that to which it is like, yet every creature has a likeness to something which it nevertheless is not, it seems that every creature is something false. But if this is true, is man, who is the likeness and image of God, and still is not God, a false God, as the statue of a man is a false man?

—ROBERT GROSSETESTE

When the Unreal Is Real

A thing cannot have a property unless it is there to have it, and, since unicorns . . . *do* have the property of being thought of, there certainly must be such things. When I think of a unicorn, what I am thinking of is certainly not nothing; if it were nothing, then, when I think of a griffin, I should also be thinking of nothing and there would be no difference between thinking of a griffin and thinking of a unicorn. But there certainly is a difference; and what can the difference be except that in one case what I am thinking of is a unicorn. and in the other a griffin? And if the unicorn is what I am thinking of, then there certainly must *be* a unicorn, in spite of the fact that unicorns are unreal. In other words, though in one sense of the words there certainly *are* no unicorns—that sense, namely, in which to assert that there are would be equivalent to asserting that unicorns are real—yet there must be some other sense in which there *are* such things, since, if there were not, we could not think of them.

—G. E. Moore

Edward von Hartmann objected to the existence of God on the ground that, if He were conscious, he would go mad trying to understand the mystery of His own existence.

F. C. S. Schiller said that there "are puzzles which arise from the natural practice of *revaluing* superseded 'truths' as 'errors,' and of *antedating* the new truths as having been 'true all along.' So it may be asked 'What were these truths *before* they were discovered?' "

But Schiller added that the difficulty is merely verbal.

That Stupidity Is Essential For the
Preservation of Freedom

I fear you will laugh when I tell you what I conceive to be about the most essential mental quality for a free people whose liberty is to be progressive, permanent, and on a large scale: it is much stupidity. . . .

What we opprobiously call "stupidity," though not an enlivening quality in common society, is nature's favorite resource for preserving steadiness of conduct and consistency of opinion; it enforces concentration: people who learn slowly learn only what they must. The best security for people's doing their duty is that they should not know anything else to do; the best security for fixedness of opinion is that people should be incapable of comprehending what is to be said on the other side. . . .

What I call proper stupidity . . . chains the gifted professor mainly to his old ideas: it takes him seven weeks to comprehend an atom of a new one; it keeps him from being led away by new theories, for there is nothing which bores him so much; it restrains him within his old pursuits, his well-known habits, his tried expedients, his verified conclusions, his traditional beliefs. He is not tempted to levity or impatience, for he does not see the joke and is thick-skinned to present evils. Inconsistency puts him out. "What I say to this here, as I was saying yesterday," is his notion of historical eloquence and habitual discretion. He is very slow indeed to be excited—his passions, his feelings, and his affections are dull and tardy strong things, failing in a certain known direction, fixed on certain known objects, and for the most part acting in a moderate degree and at a sluggish pace. You always know where to find his mind.

—WALTER BAGEHOT

Many years ago Lady Viola Welby offered to pay one thousand pounds to any philosopher who could produce adequate documentary evidence that he:

1. Knows what he means
2. Knows what anyone else means
3. Knows what everyone means
4. Knows what anything means
5. Knows what everything means
6. Means what he says
7. Means what he means
8. Means what everyone else means
9. Means what everyone else says that he means
10. Can express what he means
11. Knows what it signifies what he means
12. Knows what it matters what he signifies

It is commonly supposed that it is always better to be somewhat right than never right. But this is by no means true. For example, consider the case of a watch which has stopped; it is exactly right twice every day. A watch, on the other hand, which is always five minutes slow is never exactly right. And yet there can be no question but that a belief in the accuracy of the watch which was never right would, on the whole, produce better results than such a belief in the one which had altogether stopped.

—P. E. B. JOURDAIN

Determinism

There is no free will in the human mind: it is moved
to this or that volition by some cause, and that cause
has been determined by some other cause, and so on
infinitely.

—BARUCH SPINOZA

If the theory of determinism is true, then no arguments against it have any force. But then, if it is true,
no arguments in its favor have any force either. It is
pretty clear that no one in normal society in fact holds
this position in its fullness, for its consistent adoption
would lead to insanity.

—E. L. MASCALL

The falsity of determinism lies simply in the dogma
that the future is already determinate. But if this were
so there would be no future; the future would be already past.

—JOHN MACMURRAY

I V

Math and Economics
Guyed

The Fifty-cent Barrel of Whiskey

George and John owned a tavern located at a small crossroads community. One day they ran out of whiskey and together they drove into town to buy another barrel of it.

On the way back to the tavern each man's mouth watered for a drink of the whiskey, but each hesitated to suggest they violate their mutual agreement not to partake of it.

Finally, George pulled a half-dollar from his pocket and said, "John, I'd like to buy myself a drink of that whiskey."

John, being a good merchant, could not turn down a sale. But presently John's thirst got the better of him and he used the same half-dollar to buy himself a drink from George.

For the balance of the journey back to the tavern George and John kept on buying drinks for themselves with the same half-dollar until almost all of the whiskey was gone.

"Ish marvelous," chortled George, "between us we got a whole barrel of whiskey for a half-dollar."

The Mathematics of the Lost Chord

Everyone is familiar with the melodious yet melancholy song of "The Lost Chord." It tells us how, seated one day at the organ, weary, alone and sad, the player let his fingers roam idly over the keys, when suddenly, strangely, he "struck one chord which echoed like the sound of a Great Amen."

But he could never find it again. And ever since then there have gone up from myriad pianos the mournful laments for the Lost Chord. Ever since then, and this happened eighty years ago, wandering fingers search for the Lost Chord. No musician can ever find it.

But the trouble with the musicians is that they are too dreamy, too unsystematic. Of course they could never find the Lost Chord by letting their fingers idly roam over the keys. What is needed is *method*, such as is used in mathematics every day. So where the musician fails let the mathematician try. He'll find it. It's only a matter of time.

The mathematician's method is perfectly simple— a matter of what he calls Permutations and Combinations—in other words, trying out all the Combinations till you get the right one.

He proposes to sound all the Combinations that there are, listen to them, and see which is the Great Amen. Of course a lot of the combinations are not chords at all. They would agonize a musician. But the mathematician won't notice any difference. In fact the only one he would recognize is Amen itself, because it's the one when you leave church.

He first calculates how many chords he can strike

in a given time. Allowing time for striking the cord, listening to it and letting it die away, he estimates that he can strike one every 15 seconds, or 4 to a minute, 240 to an hour. Working 7 hours a day with Sundays off and a half-day off on Saturday, and a short vacation (at a summer school in Mathematics) he reaches the encouraging conclusion that *if need be*—if he didn't find the Chord sooner—he could sound away as many as half a million chords within a single year!

The next question is how many combinations there are to strike. The mournful piano player would have sat strumming away for ever and never have thought that out. But it's not hard to calculate. A piano has 52 white notes and 36 black ones. The player can make a combination by striking 10 at a time (with all his fingers and thumbs), or any less number down to 2 at a time. Moreover he can, if a trained player, strike any 10, adjacent or distant. Even if he has to strike notes at the extreme left and in the middle and at the extreme right all in the same combination, he does it by rapidly sweeping his left hand towards the right, or his right towards the left. There is a minute fraction between the initial strokes of certain notes, but not enough to prevent them sounding together as a combination.

This makes the calculation simplicity itself. It merely means calculating the total combinations of 88 things, taken 2 at a time, 3 at a time and so on up to 10 at a time.

The combinations, 2 notes at a time,

Are $\dfrac{88 \times 87}{1 \times 2}$ 3,828

For 3 at a time $\dfrac{88 \times 87 \times 86}{1 \times 2 \times 3}$ 109,736

For 4 at a time $\dfrac{88 \times 87 \times 86 \times 85}{1 \times 2 \times 3 \times 4}$ 2,331,890

For 5 at a time $\dfrac{88 \times 87 \times 86 \times 85 \times 84}{1 \times 2 \times 3 \times 4 \times 5}$ 39,175,750

For 6 at a time $\dfrac{88 \times 87 \times 86 \times 85 \times 84 \times 83}{1 \times 2 \times 3 \times 4 \times 5 \times 6}$ ...541,931,236

For 7 at a time $\dfrac{88 \times 87 \times 86 \times 85 \times 84 \times 83 \times 82}{1 \times 2 \times 3 \times 4 \times 5 \times 6 \times 7}$

....6,348,337,336

For 8 at a time $\dfrac{88 \times 87 \times 86 \times 85 \times 84 \times 83 \times 82 \times 81}{1 \times 2 \times 3 \times 4 \times 5 \times 6 \times 7 \times 8}$

....64,276,915,527

For 9 at a time $\dfrac{88 \times 87 \times 86 \times 85 \times 84 \times 83 \times 82 \times 81 \times 80}{1 \times 2 \times 3 \times 4 \times 5 \times 6 \times 7 \times 8 \times 9}$

....571,350,360,240

For 10 at a time $\dfrac{88 \times 87 \times 86 \times 85 \times 84 \times 83 \times 82 \times 81 \times 80 \times 79}{1 \times 2 \times 3 \times 4 \times 5 \times 6 \times 7 \times 8 \times 9 \times 10}$

....4,513,667,845,896

For all combinations 5,156,227,011,439

This gives us then an honest straightforward basis on which to start the search. The player setting out at his conscientious pace of half a million a year has the consoling feeling that he may find the Great Amen first shot, and at any rate he's certain to find it in 10,000,000 years.

It's a pity that the disconsolate players were so easily discouraged. The song was only written eighty years ago; they've hardly begun. Keep on, boys.

—STEPHEN LEACOCK

A fifty-year-old man married a thirty-year-old woman. When asked how a marriage with such an age differential worked out, he said: "It really works out very well. When she looks at me she feels ten years older. When I look at her I feel ten years younger. So then we're both forty."

2 equals 1, since 2 minus 2 equals 1 minus 1.

But Where Did They Get the Coal?

Three men with the merest smattering of arithmetic were employed by a coal yard and told to deliver to 7 families equal quantities of coal from a lot of 28 tons.

The first man argued that if there were seven families and 28 tons, then you divide 28 by 7, and this is the way he did it: seven into 8 is 1, leaving 21, and 7 into 21 is 3, which makes 13 tons to each family.

The second man, impressed by the first man's complex skill, argued that there was an easier way. He said that one should add 13 seven times. So he put down 13 seven times, each under the other, then he started from the bottom of the 3 column and added to the top, reaching a total of 21. Then he went down the 1 column, adding each 1 to the 21 total he got from the 3 column, and he ended up with a total of 28—thus proving to his own satisfaction that 7 times 13 is 28.

The third man, a skeptic, wanted to prove these calculations. He thought that if you could multiply 13 by 7 and get 28, then all would be well. To prove this out, he said that 7 times 3 is 21, and 7 times 1 is 7, which makes 28, and then agreed it would be correct to deliver 13 tons to each of the families.

And that is exactly what they did, but no one has ever been able to find out how it was accomplished.

F. C. S. Schiller said that even in abstract arithmetic, experience is a factor, and that the statement "two and two make four" is always incomplete because one has to know to what twos and fours the statement applies. It would not, he said, for example be true of lions and lambs, nor of drops of water, nor of pleasures and pains.

How Many Apples Did Adam and Eve Eat?

We know that Eve 81, and that Adam 812, totaling 893. But Adam 8142 please his wife, and Eve 81242 please Adam, totaling 89,384. Then again Eve 814240 fy herself, and Adam 8124240 fy himself, totaling 8,938,480.

Grand Total: 9,028,757

Tricking a Thief

A New England merchant arrived in New York City and registered at a midtown hotel. Before going to his room he handed the clerk at the desk a one hundred dollar bill and asked him to keep it in the hotel safe for him. When he asked for the return of the bill the next morning the hotel clerk denied he had ever been given it. "You have no receipt for it and I have no record of having it," he said.

Later in the day the New Englander related his experience to a friend. "I've an idea," said his friend. And so several hours later the hotel guest gave the clerk another hundred dollar bill to be held in the safe for him. But this time the New Englander had his friend with him to witness the action.

The next morning the guest went again to the desk and asked for the return of his one hundred dollar bill. The clerk gave it to him immediately, realizing the guest now could produce a witness that the bill had been given to him.

Later in the day the guest returned to the hotel with his friend and demanded the return of the one hundred dollar bill left with him the previous afternoon. The second hundred dollar bill was returned without comment.

James Finan writes, in *The Reader's Digest* for July, 1942:

"Maybe figures can't lie, but liars can certainly figure, and that's why statistics can be made to "prove" almost anything. Consider a group of ten girls: nine of them virgins, one pregnant.

"On the 'average,' each of the nine virgins is 10 per cent pregnant, while the girl who's about to have the baby is 90 per cent a virgin."

The Mousetrap Myth

Recently, while surveying the investment possibilities of the mousetrap industry, I began to wonder if Ralph Waldo Emerson knew what he was talking about when he said: "If a man builds a better mousetrap, though he build his house in the woods, the world will make a beaten path to his door."

Emerson's remark suggested that the company making the best mousetrap should pay the biggest dividends because it wouldn't have to spend a cent on salesmen or advertising. Customers would beat a path to its door.

If this sounds blue skyish, let me cite figures that Emerson did not have when he was going around the nation pleading for better mousetraps.

In 1960 there were 55,189,000 households in the U. S. Every household presumably has a pair of mice sometime during the year.

A pair of mice means there are going to be more of them. They are neither celibate nor inhibited. Married mice will have about 36 children a year, given compatibility, good food, and health.

When each mouse is four months old it too goes into production—or reproduction—and it begins to have its 36 children each year despite, or maybe because of, its youth. Consequently, within one year a pair of compatible mice will have multiplied to 686. (In two years they will total 65,778.)

This, mind you, in a single household. On a national scale it adds up to 23,870,000,000 mice in American households in one year.

The mouse, I concluded from this data, is a major

problem. Every household needs mousetraps, and people have continually to replace those they have discarded when mice are caught in them.

There is clearly a constant need for 11,037,800,000 new mousetraps every year in the U. S. alone. The production of traps has to keep up with the reproduction of the mice. You have continually to catch at least the new mice that keep coming along—say about 200 per household, after making liberal allowances for illness, malnutrition, sterility, and cats.

It seemed to offer tremendous profit possibilities for the maker of the better mousetrap.

If a man makes a better mousetrap he should capture at least 60 per cent of the market without beckoning to a single customer—or mouse. That means he should sell about 6,600,000,000 mousetraps a year. Since he would have no sales or advertising costs (because the world would beat a path to his door), and since with the best product he could charge a little more for it, he should net at least one cent per trap, or a $66 million profit before taxes.

Naturally, the next step was to ferret out the best maker of mousetraps.

It was then that I first began to wonder if Emerson was really a major prophet. I was unable to find the stock of a single manufacturer of mousetraps listed on any of the nation's stock exchanges, or even in the over-the-counter market. It was a blow to discover that the making of mousetraps was not important or profitable enough to merit the stature of a listed stock.

At first I though someone might have invented such a fine mousetrap that he put himself and the mice out of business. But then I realized that I still see and hear mice—and women screaming when *they* see them.

I next consulted a big directory of American manufacturers, and found only sixteen companies listed as engaged in the manufacture of mousetraps; whereas seventeen companies make fly traps, and literally hundreds of outfits make all kinds of plumbing traps, which raises the question as to whether plumbers are a greater menace than mice—or is there some kind of sport involved in the trapping of plumbers? Anyway —and here was the real shock—ten of these makers of mousetraps appear to engage in it only as a sideline. The other six companies are all quite small, having capital less than $10,000.

Obviously, the making of mousetraps is pretty small potatoes as things go these days. Americans are more interested in television, automobiles, cigarettes, and Communism. Yet the mice keep on increasing. It is their occupation.

Possibly the fault is that not one of these companies comes right out and says that it makes mousetraps. One titles itself as an animal trap company, another a rat trap company, and the others conceal the nature of their business behind surnames or such terms as Wireworks and Metal Stamping. Incidentally, half of these companies are located in small towns, thus reasonably complying with the Emersonian edict that they must be located in the woods if they are to be successful.

Although disabused of the hope of a financial coup in Mousetrap Common, I had by this time developed an academic interest in the problem of Mice *vs.* Men. What, I began to ask, are we doing about the mouse menace? Specifically, has any man recently invented a better mousetrap?

The U. S. Patent Office annual Index of Patents revealed that during a recent three-year period only eleven patents were issued for mousetraps. I examined the drawings and specifications of seven of these and found they are little more than variations and alleged improvements of the familiar and commonly used spring-jaw type of trap. Some of them can be set without danger to one's fingers. This is an improvement, but hardly revolutionary. Others allow release of the late mouse without having to touch it; another is supposed to be more sensitive to touch and surer in execution. One inventor proposed the substitution of rubber bands for the usual steel wire. This latter has all the earmarks of subversion and appeasement; it coddles the mouse and borders on the sentimental. Certainly none of these inventions is at all close to what Emerson had in mind.

Further investigation revealed that earlier generations of Americans paid scant attention to Emerson. In 1900 only one mousetrap patent was issued; in 1901, only two; in 1931, three; in 1934, two.

At this discouraging point I abandoned my investigation. I decided that the American people have lost the spirit of enterprise. Yankee ingenuity is now but a hollow echo out of the past. We have capitulated to the mouse.

However, since the mouse is here to stay—and stay in increasing numbers if biology and geometrical progression mean anything—I am thinking of investing in a cheese company. If the mice are not going to be exterminated, then they are going to have to be fed— and they love cheese!

—RALPH L. WOODS

Why Work?

A young fellow who did not much enjoy working engaged in some work figuring out that eventually every day will be a holiday:

Every year has 365 days.

If you sleep 8 hours a day, you use up 122 days, thus leaving 243 days.

If you rest 8 hours a day, you use up another 122 days, thus leaving 121 days.

There are 52 Sundays, thus leaving 69 days.

If you have a half-day off on every Saturday, you use up 26 days, thus leaving 43 days.

If you have 1½ hours for lunch every work day, you use up 28 days, thus leaving 15 days.

A two-week vacation equals 14 days.

This leaves only one day.

And on Labor Day nobody works.

S. Evershamen, using 60 years as the average life expectation, made the following calculation of a man's net working time:

	YEARS
Childhood, school, high school, college, university	24
Sleeping—8 hours per day	20
Vacation, weekends, holidays (73 days per year)	12
Unspeakable necessities—1½ hours per day	1.25
Feeding time in hours per day	2.5
	59.75 years

NET WORKING TIME 0.25 YEARS

A *Fun Raiser*

One of the young men in a factory was chosen to raise funds among the employees and buy a wedding present for the boss. The employee collected 25¢ from each of the 2,000 workers, and with the $500 he bought 2,000 pacakages of cigarettes, the kind with a gift coupon in each package.

He then traded the coupons in for a silver coffee service. That was the boss's wedding present. Then he gave each employee a pack of cigarettes.

When the president of the firm heard about this he decided he could use a man with such ingenuity in management. But before the boss could get around to interviewing the employee the young fellow had taken off on a vacation—with a complete fishing outfit obtained with the 5,000 trading stamps he received when he bought the cigarettes.

—SAM PAVLOVIC

Statistics

Darrell Huff, in his revealing *How to Lie With Statistics,* shows how to gross $22,500 a year.
1. Acquire at least 1 wife and 13 children.
2. Calculate the U. S. per capita income
   [$1,500 per year, at the time].
3. Multiply $1500 by 15 and it equals $22,500.

Percentages can be deceptive, said Darrell Huff in pointing to a statement years ago when Johns Hopkins University began to admit women students: "Thirty-three and one-third per cent of the women at Hopkins married faculty members!"

But it developed that at the time there were only three women enrolled at the university, and *one* of them married a member of the faculty.

Mr. Huff refers to an advertisement: "Buy your Christmas presents now and save 100 per cent," and he reminds us that the reduction is really only 50 per cent. A 100 per cent reduction from the original price would be a giveaway. The advertised 100 per cent reduction was not from the original price, but rather was based on the reduced new price. And when the head of a flower growers' association said "Flowers are 100 per cent cheaper than four months ago," he was saying, but not meaning, that florists were giving the flowers away.

A speaker, warning against the pitfalls of statistics, pointed out that the families of Princeton graduates average 1.8 children, whereas for Smith graduates the figure was 1.4. He added, "A faulty conclusion could be drawn from these figures: that men have more children than women."

One of the Ways Arithmetic

Used to Be Taught

When first the Marriage Knot was tied
   Between my wife and me,
My age did her's as far exceed
   As three Times three does three;
But when ten years, and Half Ten years,
   We Man and Wife had been,
Her age came up as near to mine
   As eight is to sixteen.
Now tell me, I pray,
   What were our Ages in the Wedding Day?
                (1771)

Dr. Thomas Banks Strong tells of Lewis Carroll's attempts to solve common sense problems by mathematics or logic. Sometimes he would ask his class at Christ Church, "If it takes ten men so many days to build a wall, how long will it take 300,000 men?" Invariably some members of the class would give a very small figure as an answer, and Carroll's hope of finding an undergraduate who could see what he was driving at was never fulfilled. In mild despair he would say, "You don't seem to have observed that that wall would go up like a flash of lightning, and that most of those men could not have got within a mile of it."

Prospectus of the Famous Lacon, Illinois, Cat-and-Rat Ranch

GLORIOUS OPPORTUNITY TO GET RICH—We are starting a cat ranch in Lacon with 100,000 cats. Each cat will average twelve kittens a year. The cat skins will sell for thirty cents each. One hundred men can skin 5,000 cats a day. We figure a daily net profit of over $10,000. Now what shall we feed the cats? We will start a rat ranch next door with 1,000,000 rats. The rats will breed twelve times faster than the cats. So we will have four rats to feed each day to each cat. Now what shall we feed the rats? We will feed the rats the carcasses of the cats after they have been skinned. Now get this! We feed the rats to the cats and the cats to the rats and get the skins for nothing. [This hoax was carried by every newspaper in the U.S. in 1875.]

Who Paid For the Beer?

Some years ago a U. S. dollar was worth only 90 cents in Mexico, and a Mexican dollar worth only 90 cents in the U. S. A shrewd cowboy, aware of this exchange situation, went into a bar in Mexico, bought a ten-cent beer, paid for it with a Mexican dollar and requested he receive as change an American dollar, worth ninety cents there. He drank his beer, strolled across the border into an American bar, ordered a ten-cent beer, paid for it with the American dollar and requested a Mexican dollar in change. He returned across the border to the Mexican bar, ordered another beer—and he kept crossing and recrossing the border and drinking beers all day long. He ended the day not only full of beer but with the same amount he had when he began his beer binge.

It never occurred to the cowboy to ask: *Who paid for the beer?*

A man deposited fifty dollars in the bank, then began drawing it out over a period in various sums. When he had recovered his original fifty dollars he discovered he still had one dollar left in the account, though it had drawn no interest. Someone in the bank had ledgered it this way:

Withdraws $20, leaving balance of $30

"	15	"	"	"	15
"	9	"	"	"	6
"	6	"	"	"	0
Totals:	$50.00				$51.00

If a cat can kill a rat in a minute, how long would it be killing 60,000 rats? Ah, how long indeed! My private opinion is, that the rats would kill the cat.

—LEWIS CARROLL

When accepting the National Football Foundation and Hall of Fame's gold medal for his alma mater, Roger Blough, chairman of U. S. Steel, said: "In the three years I played, we won six, lost seventeen, and tied two. Some statistician with a great capacity for charity has calculated that we won 75 per cent of the games we didn't lose."

How To Please Industry

David Ricardo, famous English economist (1772–1823), promulgated a law of wages that delighted employers. He stated that the price of labor rises and falls with demand; when demand is slight, wages remain at the bare-subsistence level. Then when labor demand increases, wages go up, workers have more money, and consequently they produce more children. This increase in population in turn pushes wages down to the subsistence level again. So what's the use of trying to improve the conditions of the workers?

Nassau Senior, English economist (1790–1864), argued that it was impossible to reduce the hours of labor (then often sixty-eight hours a week) because the employer's profit came only from the last hour of production. Eliminate that hour and you eliminate profits, and thus ruin a nation's economy.

The Check That Didn't Bounce

A dentist spotted a deadbeat patient while dining at his country club one evening. He called the patient aside, reminded him that he owed him $250 for work done more than two years earlier, and insisted the man pay up. To the dentist's astonishment, the patient pulled a checkbook from his pocket and wrote a check to the dentist for the full amount.

Skeptical about the patient's good faith, the dentist went directly to the bank the next morning and presented the check for payment. The teller handed it back with the explanation that the patient's account was a little short of the amount of the check. Following a few minutes of good-natured conversation the dentist learned that the man's account was twenty-five dollars short of the needed amount. The dentist smiled, went to the customers' desk for a few minutes, came back to the teller, deposited thirty dollars to the account of the patient, and then again presented the check for $250 and walked out with a net gain of $220.

Government Regulations

We request that every hen lay 130 to 140 eggs a year. The increase can not be achieved by the bastard hens (non-Aryan) which now populate German farm yards. Slaughter these undesirables and replace them.
>
>—Nazi Party News Agency, April 3, 1937

Cows or cattle which were bought from Jews directly or indirectly may not be bred with the community bull.
>
>—Mayor of Koenigsdorf, Bavaria, October, 1935

Two men bet on who could eat the most oysters. One man ate ninety-nine, but the other ate one hundred and won. Did the winner eat one or two more oysters than the loser?

"I have two and a half dozen children," one man said to the other.

"Good Lord, what a family!" exclaimed the listener.

"Oh, it's really not so bad. Two, and a half dozen which is six, makes eight. I have eight children, as I said."

HE Would you lend me ten dollars if I asked you?

SHE Why, certainly I would.

HE O.K., then lend me ten but just give me five dollars.

SHE All right, but why only five?

HE Then you'll owe me five, and I'll owe you five, and we'll be even.

It is an undeniable fact that, if a fox terrier two feet long, with a tail an inch and a half high, can dig a hole three feet deep in 10 minutes, to dig the Panama Canal in a single year would require only one fox terrier 15 miles long, with a tail a mile and a half high. This is statistically true; yet one must seriously consider whether, after finding the fox terrier, one could make it mind.

—BURGES JOHNSON

Verbal Victory

It has been reported that at the Brussel's World's Fair the confident Russians asked a Swiss engineer to make a professional comparison between a small Russian automobile and an American compact car. After exhausitive tests the engineer rated the American car first and the Russian car second. Crestfallen but undaunted, the Russian press reported that "in a competition between a Russian car and foreign cars, the Russian car stood second and the American car was next to last."

A woman, asked her age when applying for a passport, replied: "Let me explain it this way. I was eighteen when I married my husband, who was then thirty. He is now sixty, or twice as old as he was then, so I must be thirty-six."

The Circular Economy

Rags make paper, paper makes money, money makes banks, banks make loans, loans make poverty, poverty makes rags.

TEACHER What is half of eight?
PUPIL Which way?
TEACHER What do you mean?
PUPIL I mean, on top or sideways.
TEACHER What difference does that make?
PUPIL Well, the top half of eight is zero, but the half on one side is three.

Who's Ahead?

Russia mines gold. Russia sells the gold to the U. S. and with the proceeds buys gold-mining machinery from the U. S. With that machinery she mines more gold, which is sold to the U. S. for more gold-mining machinery, for more gold, and so on.

Joe Gyp took a five dollar bill to a pawn shop and pawned it for three dollars. Then he sold the pawn ticket to Joe Dope for three dollars. Mr. Dope thereupon took the pawn ticket to the pawn shop, redeemed it for the five dollar bill, and walked happily away in the belief that he had made himself two dollars. No one had the cruelty to tell him he had paid six dollars for the five dollar bill, since he had to pay another three dollars when he turned in the pawn ticket.

Accountants Can't Agree On This

A merchant begins business with one pair of shoes, which cost him $5.00. During his first year in business there are several price advances, but he always receives enough when he sells one pair of shoes to pay all his expenses and buy another pair of shoes to sell.

At the end of the year he has one pair of shoes left, which cost him $8.00 because of higher prices. Upon figuring his income for the year he finds he has a profit of $3.00, or the difference in price between the pair of shoes he started with and pair he has on hand at the close of the year. Out of this $3.00 he will have to pay an income tax of $1.00.

But then someone tells him that he can avoid payment of this $1.00 income tax if he puts his inventory on a "last-in-first-out" basis, which allows for the reduced purchasing power of the dollar insofar as it has been reflected in actual transactions.

In other words, the first method reflects monetary income, and the second method reflects economic—or purchasing power—income.

Which is the better method for the merchant? Is he really better off by $2.00 by the first method than he was at the beginning of the year?

Some accountants say that the merchant has made a real profit if he can sell the last pair of shoes for more than he paid for it. Other accountants assert that if the increased price of the shoes is generally indicative of prices in general, then the merchant is no better off than when he started in business because he cannot buy more with the $8.00 he would get for the last pair of shoes than he could buy with the $5.00 he had at the beginning of the year.

Two men were asked to appraise the value of a horse which was actually worth $100. One man valued the horse at $10, and the other man said it was worth $1,000. Then the question arose as to which appraiser was wider of the mark.

A geometrician said that both appraisals were *equally* wrong because the ratio of 1,000 to 100 is the same as 100 to 10.

A hard-headed businessman laughed at such a conclusion and said the greater error was the $1,000 appraisal because the excess of $1,000 above $100 is greater than that of $100 above $10.

The Moscow Radio announced that five million Russians filed past Josef Stalin's bier in seventy-two hours. That means, according to the calculations of Frank Baker, a Mangum, Oklahoma, accountant, that the mourners, two abreast, three and one-third feet apart, ran past the bier at twenty-two miles an hour. Twenty-two miles an hour is 9.3 seconds a hundred yards, which is the world's record for the hundred-yard dash, recorded only by America's Mel Patton.

—Associated Press, 1953

How Old Is Anne?

This question stirred up a nationwide debate that went on for years. It appeared in the New York *Press*, in 1903.

Brooklyn, October 12

Dear Tip:

Mary is 24 years old. She is twice as old as Anne was when she was as old as Anne is now. Hold old is Anne now? A says the answer is 16; B says 12. Which is correct?

John Mahon

"No matter how I figure I can't make ends meet," said Jones.

"What is the breakdown on your spending?" asked Smith.

"It breaks down like this," replied Jones. "Forty per cent for food, 30 per cent for shelter, 20 per cent for clothing, 10 per cent for liquor, and 20 per cent for amusement and miscellaneous."

"But that adds up to 120 per cent," observed Smith.

"That's just it," said Jones.

Charles Lamb asked a friend for a loan of five shillings. But the friend had only half-a-crown, which he gave to Lamb.

Some time later the friend encountered Lamb and said, "By the way, you owe me half-a-crown."

"Oh, no," replied Lamb. "In fact you owe me; I asked you for a crown and you only gave me half. You still owe me the other half."

Theologiae Christianae Principia Mathematica, Auctore Johanne Craig, London, 1699 . . . This is a celebrated speculation, and has been reprinted abroad, and seriously answered. Craig is known in the early history of fluxions, and was a good mathematician. He professed to calculate, on the hypothesis that the suspicions against historical evidence increase with the square of the time, how long it will take the evidence of Christianity to die out. He finds, by formulae, that had it been oral only, it would have gone out A. D. 800; but, by the aid of the written evidence, it will last till A. D. 3150. At this period he places the second coming, which is deferred until the extinction of evidence, on the authority of the question, "When the Son of Man cometh, shall he find faith on the earth?" It is a pity that Craig's theory was not adopted; it would have spared a hundred treatises on the end of the world, founded on no better knowledge than his.

—Augustus De Morgan

The Successful Ignoramus

Two young men who had majored in economics and taken post-graduate courses in Management started their own business to put into practice all that they had learned in college. But before long they were bankrupt and an unlettered fellow took over the business. The two educated men felt sorry for their successor and told him all they knew of economic and management theory as it applied to the business.

Some time later the two former proprietors stopped in to see how their successor was doing, and they were astonished to learn that the business was booming and highly profitable.

"How did you do it?" they asked.

"Well," said the man without an education, "I have no education and so all the theory you fellows told me was wasted. So I just had to operate by buying an article for one dollar and selling it for two dollars. I have had to be satisfied with a one percent profit."

Population Explosion Exploded

Paul Tabori reports that *Almanach of Gotha*, a German publication that published data on royal and titled families, listed the Maharajah of Lahore, Randsit Singh, as having 18,183 children when he was age 36. The *Almanach* gave no details of the Maharajah's wives, but when he died he left at least four wives and seven concubines.

Several skeptics took out pencil and paper and began to figure: If the Maharajah first became a father at age 16, then 7,300 days would pass by the time he reached age 36. This means that he had to father 2½ children *each day* from age 16 to age 36. How many wives or concubines he would have had to have is quite another calculation. It is known that the Maharajah really did have 183 children, which in itself is not a bad record.

When Smith won a huge lottery prize with number 54 he was congratulated by his friend Jones. "How come you picked number 54?" Jones asked.

"I saw it in a dream. Seven sevens appeared to me in my sleep and they wouldn't go away. So when I woke up I remembered this and said seven times seven is 54—so I choose number 54—and won."

"But seven times seven is not 54!" cried Jones in exasperation.

"O.K., O.K.," retorted Smith. "You be the mathematician."

•

Consoling Analysis

A politician was enraged when he read what he regarded as a slanderous attack on his character and competence.

But one of his friends urged him to calm down and consider the matter analytically. "Bear in mind," said the friend, "there are 20,000 people in this town. One half of them don't get this paper. That leaves 10,000. One-half of those who get the paper didn't see the story; that leaves 5,000. One-half of those who saw it don't believe it. That leaves 2,500. One-half of those who believe it don't know you. That leaves 1,250. One-half of those who know you are your friends. That leaves 625. One-half of those felt that way about you before they read the story. So there's really nothing to get excited about."

●

Trading Tricks

A Yankee ship arrived with a cargo of woodenware at a Virginia port, unloaded it, and decided to buy some livestock then on sale. There was a lot of twenty-one hogs—seven of them fine and fat, averaging two hundred pounds each, another seven averaging one hundred pounds each, and the third seven about fifty pounds each.

The captain bid for first choice of seven hogs at seven dollars per hundredweight. The mate bid for seven of the remaining fourteen at one dollar per hundred pounds. A sailor took those left at fifty cents per hundred pounds.

When delivery of the hogs was made to the ship, the captain amazed the dealers by choosing the seven leanest hogs. The mate then exercised his second choice by selecting the seven next-leanest. The sailor took the seven fattest hogs.

And so the Yankees sailed away, happy in the knowledge that had they chosen according to the usual method the twenty-one hogs would have cost them $106.75 whereas they paid only a total of $38.50.

An uninitiated or unthinking pork dealer bargained with a wily hog raiser for the purchase of one-half of a certain lot of hogs that the hog raiser was taking into town. They agreed that the transfer of the hogs would be made at the bridge entering town, the dealer to take delivery when exactly one-half of the hogs had stepped on the bridge.

On the appointed day at the appointed hour the hog raiser came down the road toward the bridge, and as he neared the point of transfer he drove the creatures onto the bridge at a gallop. When exactly one-half of the hogs stepped on the bridge, the hog raiser stepped in and stopped the remaining half. The dealer was there to take delivery of the hogs that stepped on the bridge. He did not then realize that he was getting not only the swiftest hogs of the lot, but also the leanest.

A trader with a boatload of shingles arrived in Philadelphia in search of a buyer. A Quaker merchant asked what the price was.

"If you choose the bundles," replied the seller," the price is ten dollars a bundle. But if I choose the bundles, then it is ony five dollars a bundle."

"O.K., Captain," said the Quaker, "you choose the bundles and I'll buy the entire cargo."

Yankee Stratagems

P. T. Barnum told about a Yankee peddler who stopped at his grandfather's store in Bethel, Connecticut, a town then famous for its wits and jokers. The peddler offered to sell razor strops for a dollar each. "Why those Pomeroy strops will be sold for half that amount before the year is out," exclaimed the grandfather.

When the peddler promised to give the storekeeper another strop if one of them was sold for fifty cents within the year, the deal was agreed to and consummated. After receiving the strop and paying the dollar to the peddler, the grandfather turned to a bystander and said he didn't think he wanted the strop after all and offered to sell it to him for fifty cents. When the offer was accepted the peddler laughingly handed over another strop to the storekeeper, then confessed that the strops had cost him only twelve and one-half cents and customarily sold for twenty-five cents each.

Barnum also told about the experience of a Danbury, Connecticut, storekeeper who had been bested by a succession of peddlers and who had vowed to even the score. His opportunity came when a peddler whom he refused to deal with said, "I will sell you anything I have on my wagon at my wholesale price, and I will take in exchange anything you please to pay me from your store at the retail price."

The storekeeper, suddenly interested, looked over the contents of the wagon but saw nothing he wanted except a lot of whetstones, of which the peddler had a large quantity. He asked the price.

"My wholesale price of whetstones is three dollars per dozen," said the peddler.

"I'll take a gross," said the storekeeper.

When the whetstones had been counted out and handed over, the peddler said "You now owe me $36.00, which I'm to be paid in whatever merchandise you select at the retail price. What are you going to pay me in?"

"In whetstones at fifty cents each, which will take just six dozen of them," said the pleased storekeeper.

Turncoats

A clothing manufacturer found himself stuck with a large inventory of expensive fur-lined coats that had suddenly gone out of style. He billed twenty-five of his best accounts for a dozen each of the coats, and then delivered each of them thirteen coats. He was confident their cupidity would result in their paying for the twelve coats for which they were billed. However, every one of his customers returned twelve coats for credit.

The Beggar and the Buns

The clever beggar was broke and hungry, but unde-
terred by the circumstances. He went into a restaurant
and asked the waitress for two sugar buns. When they
were placed before him he looked at them and said he
had changed his mind—he would rather have two
rolls. After quickly eating the rolls the beggar got up
to leave, whereupon the waitress came up and said,
"Where's the money for the food? You haven't paid
for those rolls?"

"What are you talking about, lady? Didn't I give
you those sugar buns for two rolls—and the price is
the same for both."

"Yes," replied the waitress, "but you didn't pay for
the sugar buns."

"Of course I didn't. I didn't eat the sugar buns!"

Horse Trade

A wealthy Arab died, and his will stipulated that one-half of all his horses should go to the oldest son, one-third of his horses to his middle son, and one-ninth to his youngest son. At the time of his death, the Arab owned seventeen horses, and the sons sorely lamented the thought of carving up some of these fine Arab steeds to comply wth their father's will. As they were bewailing their plight, an itinerant Arab with a seedy old nag chanced by, and he offered the following suggestion:

"Look, boys," he said, "let's put my horse in with your father's seventeen. Then we have eighteen. You, son number one, are to get one-half of the horses; that is nine. And you, son number two, are to get one-third of the eighteen—or six horses. And you, son number three, are to get one ninth, or two. That's a grand total of seventeen and one is left over. And that's mine. So long, boys!"

—M. H. GREENBLATT

The Shrinking River

In the space of one hundred and seventy-six years the Lower Mississippi has shortened itself two hundred and forty-two miles. That is an average of a trifle over one mile and a third per year. Therefore, any calm person, who is not blind or idiotic, can see that in the old Oölitic Silurian Period, just a million years ago next November, the Lower Mississippi River was upward of one million three hundred thousand miles long, and stuck out over the Gulf of Mexico like a fishing rod. And by the same token any person can see that seven hundred and forty-two years from now the Lower Mississippi will be only a mile and three-quarters long, and Cairo [Illinois] and New Orleans will have joined their streets together, and be plodding comfortably along under a single mayor and a mutual board of aldermen. There is something fascinating about science. One gets such wholesale returns of conjecture out of such a trifling investment of fact.

—MARK TWAIN

Burton Crane, in *The New York Times* of December 22, 1952, said that he had encountered the following explanation of relativity:

"The fly tiptoeing at one foot a minute across the bald head of the brakeman staggering at three miles an hour along the top of a freight train high-balling at forty miles an hour on a world spinning at nine hundred miles an hour and chasing its orbit at eighteen and one-half miles a second in a solar system scurrying toward the Hercules constellation at twelve and one-half miles a second."

Some Imaginary Scientific References

Shadrach, C., Meshach, H., and Abednego, H. and C. An anaerobic heat resistant monoflagellate ornithine-producing sulfur non-purple bacterium isolated from the rectum of a goat. *J. Bact.*, 70: 11, 1944.

Ramakrishnamaswami Krishnamasaminama. Curvature of high-frequency ultra sound waves in distilled Indian water. *Proc. Acad. Sc.*(b) 18: 1-243, 1951.

Schitz, K., and Spitz, G. Urea excretion, growth hormone production, and caudal temperature of the 6-week-old hypophysectomized, adrenalectomized, tonsillectomized castrated albino hamster. *Proc. Soc. Exp. Biol. and Med.*, 50: 2-4, 1956.

Vaaraahaaha, Willi; Soderhor, G., Torenssen, A., and Johnson, The Fertility, osotenicity, and agility of the sperm of the gutter urchin, *Unclepsammochinus militaris. Ex. Cell Res.*, 4: 21-30, 1949.

—R. Arnold Le Win

Wilbur Glenn Voliva, of Zion, Illinois, made several trips around the world and at the end of each announced that the earth was "as flat as a pancake." In addition to predicting the end of the world for 1923, 1927, 1930, 1935, and 1943, Mr. Voliva stated that the wearing of a hat is necessary to thinking because the headpiece holds the brains in balance.

And Mr. Voliva was confident he had routed the scientists when he asked: "Where is the man who believes he can jump into the air, remaining off the earth one second, and come down to earth 193.7 miles from where he jumped up?"

I know some who cannot understand that to take
four from nothing leaves nothing.

—BLAISE PASCAL

V

Word Wonders, Oddities, and Pen Pranks

Oddities of English Words

Two eight-letter words, one of which has one syllable and the other five syllables:

strength ideality

Three letters that, placed in any order, form a word:

ear are era rae
aer (Latin for "air") rea (a river)

A six-letter word that admits of five successive elisions, leaving at each reduction a well-known word:

brandy brand bran ran an a

A six-letter word that contains six words besides itself, without transposing a letter:

herein he her here ere rein in

Two words wherein the five vowels follow in successive order:

abstemious facetious

Three five-letter words from which, if you take two letters, one remains:

stone bones money

Two words that may be pronounced quicker and shorter by making them longer:

quick short

How to spell "blind pig" with two letters:

pg

Two words, no single letter of which is pronounced:

aye eye

The first two letters of this word signify a male, the first three a female, the first four a great man, and the whole word a great woman:

heroine

If you take away the first two letters of this one-syllable word, it becomes a word of two syllables:

plague

Take one syllable from this five-syllable word, and no syllable remains:

monosyllable.

There is a three-syllable word, the first syllable of which addresses another, the second speaks of myself, and the third speaks of company. The whole word is a harbinger of hot weather.

sirius

One word may be made out of the letters:

E D O R N O W [one word]

A word containing three successive double letters:

bookkeeper

A word which, when printed in capitals, reads the same backwards, forwards, and upside down:

NOON

Two letters describe in nine letters the position of one who has been left alone in his extremity:

A *b* and one *d*

A word of six letters which can be so read that it claims to be spelled with only one:

a b used

A word which may be treated so as to affirm or disallow the use of its own initial or its final letter:

disused (d is used; disuse d)

What word of five letters is never pronounced right?

wrong

A word that denotes more in the singular than it does in the plural:

hair

There is a word of more than two letters, of which la is the middle, is the beginning, and the end, though there are but one a and one l in the word:

island

A thirteen-letter word in which the same vowel occurs four times, the same consonant six times, another twice, and another once:

senselessness

Here is a five-syllable word of eight letters, four of which are vowels:

ideality

Our longest word, with a mile between its first and last letters.

smiles

Is there a word in the English language that contains all the vowels?

Unquestionably!

What English word contains the group of letters "gnt"?

sovereignty

What word contains "roor" in it—in that order?

microorganism

A seven-letter word with five syllables:

oxyopia

There are at least six English words, each with six letters and four syllables:

Azalea myopia utopia aviary adagio acuity

What English word begins and ends with "und?"

underground

A word containing one vowel repeated six times:

indivisibility

The following words all consist of five consonants:

pygmy myrrh gypsy tryst lymph rhythm crypt

What word contains four personal pronouns?

usher

A few long words without a repetition of letters:

playgrounds dumbwaiters workmanship
republicans sympathizer

Here is a five-letter word with four consecutive vowels, the pronunciation of which is never changed by the removal of four of the letters:

queue

It has been said that there are 34,650 ways of arranging the letters of the word Mississippi. One could blame this on a computer, except that the discovery was announced prior to 1940, when computers were in their infancy and could hardly have been used either to make such a determination or to disprove it.

Cedric Adams says that you would have to count to one thousand before encountering a number with the letter A in it.

In the sentence "But me no buts," a conjunction, sometimes used as a preposition, appears first as a verb, then as a noun.

It has been asserted that there is no English word containing a double Y.

Word Gallery

In September 1960 The Reader's Digest reprinted a collection of "word pictures" from *Playboy*, suggesting that readers might like to try *their* hand at some word artistry. Quite a few people took up the challenge and then shared their creations with us. Here's a selection:

WigWams

COUGℏ

bOsOm

FiRE! *Swan*

EYE
DOC
TOR

MEASLES

cAndles

INTOX^hic ATED

SUNSET

ALMOST

TV

Satirizing Poets Addicted to the
Use of Compound Words

Lofty-brow-flourishers,
Nose-in-beard-wallowers,
Bag-and-beard-nourishers,
Dish-and-all-swallowers,
Old-cloak-investitors,
Barefoot-look-fashioners,
Night-private-feast-eaters,
Craft-lucubrationers,
Youth-cheaters, word-catcher, vain-glory-osopherers,
Such are you seekers-of-virtue philosophers.

—JOSEPH SCALIGER

Speaking of Words,

It Isn't Easy to Speak These

Aldibornontephoscophosnio is the first word of a farce titled *Grononhatonthologos, the most tragical tragedy that was ever tragedized by any company of tragedians,* by Henry Carey, published in England about two hundred years ago.

Panzoologicomineralogia is the title of a book by Lovell, a naturalist, published at Oxford in England in 1661.

Drimtaidhorickillicattan is the name of a locality on the island of Mull, Scotland.

Cryptochonchaidsyphonostomata was the title given to a play in England many years ago.

Necrobioneopaleonthydrockthonanthropopithekology is a word invented by Charles Kingsley to mean the science of life and death of men and monkeys in bygone times.

Llanfairpwllgwyngyllgerchwyrndrobwllgerdysiliogogogogoch is supposed to be the town with the longest name (60 letters). It is in Wales, Great Britain, and translated means: Church of St. Mary in a hollow of white hazel, near a rapid whirlpool and to the Tysilio's Church near to a red cave.

Honorificabilitudinitatibus is a word invented by William Shakespeare and used in his play *Love's Labor Lost*. But, of course, Shakespeare was spoofing.

Pneumonoultramicroscopicsilicovolcanokoniosis can be found in *some* dictionaries. It is a lung condition.

Chargoggagoggmanchaugagoggchaubunagungamaug is the name of a lake in Connecticut. Tradition says that it is some kind of Indian language for: "You fish on your side, I'll fish on my side, and we'll all fish in the middle."

Years ago some anonymous minor genius figured out
that "iewkngheaurrhphthewenpeighghteaps" is merely
the word "unfortunates," justified by English spelling
of similar sounds taken letter by letter, as follows:

u—iew in view
n—kn in know
f—gh in tough
o—eau in beau
r—rrh in myrrh
t—phth in pthisis
u—ewe
n—mp in comptroller
a—eigh in neigh
t—ght in light
e—ea in tea
s—ps in psalm.

Leo Rosten (LOOK, Dec. 26, 1967) deplored the many
different ways the *ee* sound is spelled in English, such
as: m*e*, f*ee*t, cl*ea*n, bel*ie*ve, dec*ei*ve, dem*e*sne, ma-
ch*i*ne, obsc*e*ne, p*eo*ple, k*ey*, C*ae*sar, *oe*ntologist, happ*y*,
*I*a.

If one thing is that, and two things are those,
Then hat in the plural should always be hose;
The masculine pronouns are he, his and him,
But imagine the feminine she, shis and sim.

If you make thirteen strokes like this:

I I I I I I I I I I I I I

and then add thirteen more strokes, you can spell

HOTTENTOT

"Ghoughphtheightteeau" spells "potato" as explained below:

> p—gh in hiccough
> o—ough in dough
> t—phth in phthisis
> a—eigh in neighbor
> t—tte in gazette
> o—eau in beau.

If an S and I and O and a U,
With an X at the end, spell Su;
And an E and a Y and E spell I,
Pray, what is a speller to do?
Then, if also an S and I and a G
And an H E D spell cide,
There's nothing much left for a speller to do
But to go and commit Siouxeyesighed.

Years ago the following won a prize in England for the Longest Twelve-Word Telegram:

ADMINISTRATOR-GENERAL'S COUNTER-REVOLUTIONARY INTER-COMMUNICATIONS UNCIRCUMSTANTIATED STOP QUARTERMASTER-GENERAL'S DISPROPORTIONABLENESS CHARACTERISTICALLY CONTRA-DISTINGUISHED UNCONSTITUTIONALIST'S INCOMPREHENSIBILITIES STOP

No one in Lord Palmerston's Cabinet could spell the following correctly when it was dictated to him: *It is disagreeable to witness the embarrassment of a harassed peddler gauging the symmetry of a peeled potato.*

In 1938 *This Week* magazine stated that if you read the following sentence to a friend and ask him to write it down, something is almost certain to get misspelled: *Outside a cemetery sat a harassed cobbler and an embarrassed oculist, picknicking on a desiccated apple, and gazing at the symmetry of a lady's ankle with unparalleled ecstasy.*

Conjugations

I am sparkling. You are unusually talkative. He is drunk.

I am beautiful. You have quite good features. She isn't bad-looking, if you like that type.

I daydream. You are an escapist. He ought to see a psychiatrist. —THE NEW STATESMAN

I am firm, you are obstinate, he is pig-headed.
—R. H. THOULESS

Time flies you cannot they pass at such irregular in-tervals makes sense when you place a comma after the word *cannot.*

If to half a dozen you add six and five hundred, the result is clear, lucid and glowing: VIVID

If is is not is and is not is is what is it is not is and what is it is is not if is not is is? Makes sense if you punctuate as follows: If "is" is not "is," and "is not" is "is," what is it "is not" is, and what is it "is" is not, if "is not" is "is"?

A man said, in speaking of the word "that," that that that that that teacher parsed, was not that that that that man requested her to analyze.

That that is is that that is not is not is not is not that it it is makes *some* sense if you add two commas, one semicolon, two periods, and one question mark, as fol-lows: *That that is, is; that that is not is not, is not. Is not that it? It is.*

Professor Ernest Brennecke of Columbia University is reported to have invented a sentence that can be made to have eight different meanings by placing the word *only* in all possible positions in the sentence:

I hit him in the eye yesterday.

When a man was criticized for the continual use of "I say" in conversation, he wrote his critic as follows:
I say, sir, I hear you say I say "I say" at every word I say.
Now, sir, although I know I say "I say" at every word I say,

still I say, sir, it is not for you to say I say "I say" at every word I say.

The following may be given four different meanings, according to the way it is punctuated:

> Bill said Carrie
> Well said Bill
> If we ever marry
> But we never will

Joseph T. Shipley observed that a semicolon and a comma would make the following statement much less astounding: *Charles the First walked and talked half an hour after his head was cut off.*

One day at Queens College a teacher put this note on his door: "Professor Tobin will not meet his classes today." An alert student came along and crossed out the first letter of the word "classes." But Dr. Tobin, who forgot his briefcase and returned to get it, looked at the decapitated word, and rubbed out the second letters as well.

When Bishop Adam de Orleton said: *"Edvardum occidere nolite timere bonum est,"* it was translated as: "Do not fear to kill Edward; it is a good thing." And so Edward was murdered. But the crime might not have been committed if it had been translated as: "Do not kill Edward; to fear is a good thing."

Cryptic counsel written on the wall of a college for women: "Young women should set good examples, for young men *will* follow them.

The shortest play is said by Walter Hart Blumenthal to be *The Exile* by Tristran Bernard. The curtain rises to reveal a mountaineer seated before the fire in his frontier cabin. There is a knock at the door, and when it is opened The Exile enters and says, "Whoever you are, have pity on a hunted man. There is a price on my head."

The mountaineer says, "How much?"

The curtain falls.

The question mark is supposed to have derived from the first and last letters of the Latin word *Quaestio*
(question), one letter placed under the other: $\frac{Q}{o}$

The exclamation point is derived from the word *Io*
(joy), written vertically: $\frac{I}{o}$

There are at least eighteen different ways of saying: "The ploughman homeward plods his weary way" ("Elegy Written in a Country Churchyard," Thomas Gray):

1. The weary ploughman homeward plods his weary way.
2. The weary ploughman plods his homeward way.
3. The homeward ploughman plods his weary way.
4. The homeward ploughman, weary, plods his way.
5. The homeward, weary ploughman plods his way.
6. The weary, homeward ploughman plods his way.
7. Homeward, the weary ploughman plods his way.
8. Homeward, weary, the ploughman plods his way.
9. Homeward, the ploughman plods his way.
10. Homeward the ploughman, weary, plods his way.
11. Weary, the homeward ploughman plods his way.
12. Homeward, the ploughman plods his way.
13. Weary, the ploughman plods his homeward way.
14. The ploughman plods his homeward, weary way.
15. The ploughman plods his weary homeward way.
16. The ploughman, homeward, weary, plods his way.
17. The ploughman, weary, homeward plods his way.
18. The ploughman, weary, plods his homeward way.

Transformations

Changing Hard into Easy, in Five Moves:
Hard, card, cart, cast, east, Easy.

Changing Hand into Foot, in Six Moves:
Hand, hard, lard, lord, ford, fort, Foot.

Changing Sin into Woe, in Three Moves:
Sin, son, won, Woe.

Changing Hate into Love, in Three Moves:
Hate, have, lave, love.

Changing Black into White, in Eight Moves:
black, slack, stack, stalk, stale, shale, whale, while, White.

Changing Cat into Dog, in Three Moves:
Cat, cot, cog, Dog.

Changing More into Less, in Four Moves:
More, lore, lose, loss, Less.

Changing Wheat into Bread, in Seven Moves:
Wheat, cheat, cheap, cheep, creep, creed, breed, Bread.

Changing Elm into Oak, in Eight Moves:
Elm, ell, all, ail, air, fir, far, oar, Oak.

Changing Elm into Oat, in Six Moves:
Elm, ely, sly, say, bay, bat, Oat.

Changing Hare into Soup, in Seven Moves:
Hare, hark, hack, sack, sock, soak, soap, Soup.

Changing Army into Navy, in Eight Moves:
Army, arms, aims, dims, dams, dame, name, nave, Navy.

—Lewis Carroll

Joseph P. Shipley calls a certain type of semantic antic a Nimble, and offers this sample of one:

How did a man get out of a locked and barred house, in which the only piece of furniture was a table?

He rubbed his hands until they were sore. Then he sawed the table in half. Two halves make a whole. He hollered through the hole until he was hoarse, then he jumped on the horse and rode away.

A Famous Latin Word-Square
of Undetermined Origin

```
S A T O R
A R E P O
T E N E T
O P E R A
R O T A S
```

Read down each column and across each line. This has been translated to read: "Arepo the sower holds the wheel to the ground."

During the Middle Ages this was popular as a charm because the letters could be transposed to spell Paternoster, with A and O remaining for alpha and omega. However, its Christian origin is questionable since the word-square was found scratched into a column at Pompeii, which was destroyed in the year A.D. 79 by the eruption of Vesuvius.

A Dialogue in Two Words

The tragedy *William Tell* was to be played in London. On the eve of the performance, an actor familiarly known as Will asked the actor taking the part of Tell whether he thought the play would tell with the critics and the public. This is the conversation that is supposed to have taken place:

WILL The question has arisen Tell, "Will Will Tell tell: Will Tell tell Will 'Will Will Tell tell?'"
TELL Tell *will* tell Will "Will Tell tell?" Will Tell *will* tell!

Did Nott Shoot Shott?

A duel was fought in Texas by Alexander Shott and John S. Nott. Nott was shot, and Shott was not. In this case it's better to be Shott than Nott. There was a rumor that Nott was not shot, but Shott avows that he shot Nott, which proves either that the shot Shott shot at Nott was not shot, or that Nott was shot notwithstanding. Circumstantial evidence is not always good. It may be made to appear on trial that the shot Shott shot Nott, or as accidents with firearms are frequent, it may be possible that the shot Shott shot shot Shott himself, in which case the whole affair would resolve itself into its original elements, and Shott would be shot and Nott would not. We think, however, that the shot Shott shot shot not Shott but Nott.

Computer Confusion

A computer designed to translate between any two languages was demonstrated to a group of interested professional people. The audience was asked to suggest a phrase for the contraption to translate. "Out of sight, out of mind" was recommended for translation. The machine promptly obeyed the instruction, translating the phrase into Russian. Then the computer was ordered to translate the same phrase from Russian back into English, It did so, and it came out "Invisible idiot." Someone then suggested for translation the phrase "The spirit is willing, but the flesh is weak." When it came back from Russian to English it read, "The vodka is strong, but the meat is rancid."

—M. H. GREENBLATT

Some Bulls—Irish and Otherwise

The chairman of a company in Ireland said at the annual meeting of directors and shareholders: "It is alleged that half of our directors do the work while the other half do nothing at all. I assure you, gentlemen, that the reverse is the case."

Jonathan Swift wrote in his first Drapier Letter: "Therefore I do most earnestly exhort you as men, as Christians, as parents, and as lovers of your country, to read this paper with the utmost attention, or to get it read to you by others."

Sir Boyle Roche, a member of the Irish House, was famous for his Bulls, such as:

"Why, Mr. Speaker, honorable members never come to this House without expecting to find their mangled remains lying on the table."

Speaking of the dangers of a French invasion: "The murderous marshal-law men would break in, cut us to mincemeat, and throw our bleeding heads upon that table to stare us in the face."

"Mr. Speaker, it is the duty of every true lover of his country to give his last guinea to save the remainder of his fortunes."

"Sir, single misfortunes never come alone, and the greatest of all national calamities is generally followed by one much greater."

When someone complained that the sergeant-at-arms should have stopped a man in the rear of the House while the sergeant was engaged in trying to catch him in front, Roche said: "Do you think the sergeant-at-arms can be, like a bird, in two places at once?"

"The progress of the times, Mr. Speaker, is such that little children who can neither walk nor talk may be seen running about the streets cursing their Maker."

"It would be better, Mr. Speaker, to give up not only a part, but, if necessary, even the whole of our Constitution, to preserve the remainder."

"Why should we put ourselves out of the way to do anything for posterity, for what has posterity done for us?" When the laughter following this outburst subsided, Roche went on to explain: "By posterity I do not mean all of our ancestors, but those who were to come immediately after them."

Serjeant Arabin, a famous London justice, offered a prisoner "a chance of redeeming a character that he had irretrievably lost."

A Bull has been defined in "bullish" terms as "a horse of another color."

"He remarked in all seriousness that it was hereditary in his family to have no children," is the example of a Bull given in *Webster's Unabridged Dictionary*.

The U.S. Census for 1870 revealed that a father (perhaps a publisher) named his five children as follows:

Imprimis
Finis
Appendix
Addendum
Erratum

When in 1856 Parliament petitioned Queen Elizabeth for the immediate execution of Mary Queen of Scots, Elizabeth replied: "If I should say that I meant not to grant your petition by my faith I should say unto you more perhaps than I mean. And if I should say that I mean to grant it, I should tell you more than it is fit for you to know. Thus I must deliver to you an answer answerless."

"Then you should say what you mean," the March Hare went on.

"I do," Alice hastily replied; "At least—at least I mean what I say—that's the same thing, you know."

"Not the same thing a bit!" said the Hatter. "Why you might as well say that 'I see what I eat' is the same thing as 'I eat what I see.'"

"You might as well say," added the March Hare, "that 'I like what I get' is the same thing as 'I get what I like.'"

"You might as well say," added the Dormouse, which seem'd to be talking in its sleep, "that 'I breathe when I sleep' is the same as 'I sleep when I breathe.'"

—Lewis Carroll

Rule for drinking: I always drink standing up because it is much easier to sit down when I get drunk standing up than it is to get standing up when I get drunk sitting down.

Are you aware that Claude Pepper is known all over Washington as a shameless extrovert? Not only that, this man is reliably reported to practice nepotism with his sister-in-law, and he has a sister who was once a Thespian in wicked New York. Worst of all, it is an established fact that Mr. Pepper, before his marriage, practiced celibacy.
—Attributed to Congressman Smathers of Florida, when running against Mr. Pepper in 1949

The bewildered laundryman could not understand why there was such a shocked response when he said, with what he thought perfect propriety, to the nun in charge of the wash: "Good morning, Sister. Have you any dirty habits?"

When a sardine fisherman was asked what disposition was made of all the fish he caught, he replied: "We eat what we can, and we can what we can't."

Artemus Ward once asked: "Did you have the measles, and if so, how many?"

A pharmacist's equivocal sign: WE DISPENSE WITH ACCURACY

An editor who insisted that "news" was plural, wired his reporter: "Are there any news?"
The reporter replied: "No. Not a new."

A scriptural text inscribed beneath a clock on a church tower in an English village: "Be ye ready, for ye know not the time."

Is one to conclude that the clock is not reliable?

Poetical Shorthand

Dawn	Each	Fair	Me	Ray
Plains	Spoke	Mine	Too	Heat
Lawn	Beech	Hair	Free	Play
Swains	Yoke	Divine	Woo	Sweet

Tune	Fields	Shades	Adieu	Farewell
Lays	Bowers	Darts	Flocks	Cows
Moon	Fields	Maids	Renew	Dell
Gaze	Flowers	Hearts	Rocks	Bough

Here, without any more ado, we have the whole history of a couple of successful rural lovers comparing notes. They issue forth in the morning, fall in the proper place and dialogue, record the charms and kindness of their respective mistresses, do justice at the same time to the fields and shades, and conclude by telling their flocks to wait as usual, while they renew their addresses under younder boughs. How easily all this is gathered from the rhymes, and how worse than useless would it be in two persons, who have such interesting avocations, to waste their precious time and the reader's in a heap of prefatory remarks, falsely called verses!

—LEIGH HUNT

Short Sentences Containing All the Letters of the Alphabet

Each letter used once:
Export my fund! Quiz black whigs.
Dumpy quiz! Whirl back fogs next.
Fritz! Quick! Land! Hew gypsum box.

Each letter used at least once:
Z. Badger: Thy vixen jumps quick at fowl.
If Jack quiz, bald nymphs grow vext.
Quick wafting zephyrs vex bold Jim.
Pack my box with five dozen liquor jugs.
Quick! Go on, Jim! Why stop lazy fox? Drive by!
A quick brown fox jumps over the lazy dog.
J. Gray, pack with my box five dozen quail.

So he, by virtue of these presents, presents presents to all comers.

I know that that that that man had had was not enough.

If I had an idea of that, that, that that that man had was not enough, I would have given him more.

"Well," cried an agitated carpenter, "of all the saws that I ever saw saw, I never saw a saw saw as this saw saws."

An athiest put up a sign reading:

GOD IS NOWHERE

Someone changed it to read:

GOD IS NOW HERE

The Authorship of *In Memoriam*

Why Shakespeare more than anybody else? The problem "Who wrote *In Memoriam?*" is one of the most interesting and most complicated in literary history; and it is safe to say that it has not hitherto received the attention it deserved. Everybody is familiar with the outlines of it. Hallam died in 1833, and the poem which professes to be his epicedium did not see the light until 1850. What is the explanation of this monstrous interval? Further, when the poem originally appeared, it was accorded a doubtful reception, and was attributed by some critics (a very significant fact) to a feminine hand. Mr. Nicolson has familiarized us with the verdict of one reviewer in particular, who suggested that it was in all probability composed by the widow of some military man. It was only later that Tennyson stepped in, claimed the poem as his own, and gave it the reputation which it holds at present. The question naturally suggests itself, did Tennyson really write it, or was he screening somebody else? If we adopt the latter view, it will be necessary to urge some sufficient motive for a literary imposition so audacious and so persistent.

One looks, naturally, for a cryptogram. And here a most impressive fact meets us at the very outset of the inquiry. Give the letters their natural value as Greek numerals: that is, make A=1, E=5, I=10, M=40, N= 50, O=70, R=100. The letters of *In Memoriam* thus work out at 10+50+40+5+40+70+100+10+1+40, cyphers which on a careful computation add up to 366, the number of days in the full year! Scarcely less significant is the result if we take the natural values of the English alphabet, starting with A=0, B=1, C=2, etc. The letters of *In Memoriam* on this reckoning give you 8+13+12+4+12+14+17+8+0+12, and these ten cyphers add up to 100! Again, if you give the vowels their natural values as a separate series, this time making A=1, E=2, etc., you find that the vowels IEIOA represent 3+2+3+4+1, cyphers which add up to the mystical number 13. Adding 100 to 13 (for want of anything better to do), you arrive at the number 113, and immediately turn to the 113th canto of the poem to see if it holds any secret for posterity. Is it possible that the cryptographer will have betrayed, by some tiny awkwardness of phrase, some tiny evidence of strained writing, the line in this canto which contains the clue?

The search is not a difficult one. Few readers of the poem can have failed to note the artificial effect of the 11th line:

A potent voice of Parliament—

why OF Parliament, instead of IN Parliament? The latter, surely, is what any author would naturally have written. Is not the change from "in" to "of" just such a change as might have been forced on him, not by any demands of literary appropriateness, but by the desire to select two particular letters *which would complete a particular message in cypher?* It might be a fresh numerical cypher, it might be merely anagrammatical. . . . One has to play with various possibilities, and then an anagram leaps quite suddenly into view. What it is we shall see later. For the present, let us simply note that the 11th line of the 113th canto of *In Memoriam* can be read anagrammatically, and when so read gives a thoroughly sensational message.

It also (as will be seen later) indicates unmistakably that it is the *last* of a series of cryptograms. As an hypothesis, then, it may be worth considering the possibility that it is the last of a series of 11, which will involve verse 1 of canto x, verse 2 of canto y, and so on. It would be easy to construct an artificial series for the purpose (e.g. 13, 23, etc.), but a natural series is not so easily arrived at. It is here that a certain amount of intricate mathematical thinking is involved, the details of which we spare the reader, giving only the conclusions. It will be seen that the series is a real and natural one, though sufficiently abstruse to be worthy of an accomplished cryptographer such as the poet we are dealing with.

It runs as follows:

$$1 = 1$$
$$* \quad * \quad *$$
$$1 \times 2 + 1 = 3$$
$$* \quad * \quad *$$
$$2 \times 2 + 2 = 6$$
$$6 \times 2 + 1 = 13$$
$$* \quad * \quad *$$
$$3 \times 2 + 3 = 9$$
$$9 \times 2 + 2 = 20$$
$$20 \times 2 + 1 = 41$$
$$* \quad * \quad *$$
$$4 \times 2 + 4 = 12$$
$$12 \times 2 + 3 = 27$$
$$27 \times 2 + 2 = 56$$
$$56 \times 2 + 1 = 113$$

Taking the formula as $xy+z$, it will be seen that y is always 2, that z is in turn, 1, 2, 1, 3, 2, 1, 4, 3, 2, 1; that x is in turn 1, 2, 3, 4, at the beginning of the division, and in the rest of the division is simply a repetition of the last total reached.

On our present hypothesis, then (for it is so far a

hypothesis) we shall expect to find a cryptogram (in the form of an anagram) in the following lines: line 1 of canto 1, line 2 of canto 3, line 3 of canto 6, line 4 of canto 13, and so on till we get to line 11 of canto 113. Let us give the results of this speculation: —

1.	1	I held it truth, wth him who sings.
3.	2	O priestess in the vaults of death.
6.	3	And common is the commonplace.
13.	4	Her place is empty, fall like these.
9.	5	So draw him home to those that mourn.
20.	6	And weep the fulness from the mind.
41.	7	Thy changes; here upon the ground.
12.	8	And leave the cliffs, and haste away.
27.	9	Nor, what may count itself as blest.
56.	10	Such splendid purpose in his eyes.
113.	11	A potent voice of Parliament.

Before we go any farther we may at once comment upon a corroborative symptom. Omit the first two and the last two of these lines, and the intervening lines give us a perfect single acrostic. It runs, "Ah Satan!" Somebody clearly felt that he or she was being tempted to violate conscience, and registered a protest in this way. We shall see that the seven lines of the acrostic have a common thread running through them.

Anagrams are slow work, and a "Word Making and Word Taking" outfit is recommended to the beginner. The letters of "I held it truth, with him who sings" yield, with a little arrangement, the following rather intriguing result: "Who is writing this? H.M. luteth hid." It was, no doubt, the word "harp" in the next line of the poem that suggested to the cryptographer the rather fanciful word "luteth." The implication is plain enough; the author of this poem is not its reputed author; somebody described as H.M. is really writing the poem, but prefers to remain hidden, that is anonymous. So far we have not much to go upon in the way of positive information; after all, there must have been plenty of people writing in 1850 who would answer to the required initials. We turn on, then, impatiently to canto 3, line 2, and are met with a startling announcement. "O priestess in the vaults of death" reads quite unmistakably "V.R.I. the poetess. Alf T. has no duties." Astounding—impossible! Yet there it is in black and white; there is no getting over the documentary evidence. English sovereigns had not yet adopted the imperial title (the Mutiny was yet to come), but already it must have been designed *in petto*. There was only one person in England who could be designated indifferently "H.M." or "V.R.I."

And yet, is it so extraordinary? Has anybody read Queen Victoria's published diaries without being conscious of a note of domesticity, a note of resignation, a note of common human pathos, which finds its very counterpart in the stanzas of *In Memoriam*? There was, after all, something to be said for the critic who suspected feminine authorship. But at that period of our history, though a woman might write poetry, a queen might not publish it. It was necessary to conceal the secret as if it had been a guilty one, or the consequences might have been international. The arrangement, then, clearly, was that the work should be published anonymously, but that Tennyson, then a rising poet, should be prepared if necessary to cast veracity to the winds, and shoulder the onus of authorship. It was a patriot's act; and perhaps something of the moral struggle which it involves is reflected in the next cryptogram, which is in Latin. "And common is the commonplace" (a line which many of us have felt before now to be something less than Elizabethan in its quality) is after all only an ingenious cloak for the Latin motto "Pie hoc nomen clam commodans. T.", that is to say, "Devotedly lending this name in secret. T." The man who wrote thus had faced a moral problem, and had risen superior to it.

It would be necessary for Tennyson to "lend his name" if either of two things happened—if discovery of the real authorship threatened, or if the anonymous appearance of the book should prove injurious to its sales. Which motive in fact became operative? The next cryptogram leaves us in no doubt, and indeed casts a rather sinister light on the whole proceeding. Tennyson had no doubt been studying Bacon as a master of cryptographic method; and he will have been struck, as all of us will have been struck, at the singular ease with which you may find cryptograms in the works of the Elizabethans, *because any sort of spelling will do*. Imitating, then, the crude orthography of Gloriana's period, he has delicately indicated the motive which was responsible, at least in part, both for the original publication of the poem and for the invocation of Tennysonian patronage. "Her place is empty, fall like these" can be nothing other than "Her Maiesty lacks pelf. I'le help. TE."

It will already have occurred to the ingenious reader that the letter T left over in the third, and the letters TE left over in the fourth cryptogram, are a sort of rudimentary signature, which (by a pretty piece of ingenuity) adds one letter to itself each time it occurs. This is true only of the seven lines which form the acrostic "Ah, Satan," and consequently they stop at "TENNYSO," just short of the complete signature. The fifth and sixth are mere repetitions of the message which the earlier cypher has given us. "So draw him home to those that mourn" is to be read (no doubt in playful allusion to the May Queen) as "O Mother, I'm H.M.'s shadow-author! TEN." "And weep the fulness from the mind" is meant for a mock warning to the reviewers of the poem, suitably couched in the words, "Who pummels Faith-Defender? TENN." One recognizes, in the choice of the verb, Tennyson's own love for vigorous English.

Alas, that our minds should be built on such a mercenary pattern! We naturally ask, was this generous loan of his name to bring Tennyson no reward from the real authoress of the poem? History supplies us with a painfully distinct answer—Tennyson became Poet Laureate in 1850, the very year of *In Memoriam's* publication! It is no doubt to this recognition of his services that he alludes, with what some will think doubtful taste, in the next cryptogram. We have done our best to find some other anagrammatic equivalent for the words "Thy changes; here upon the ground," but the unfortunate fact defeats us. There can be no doubt that we are to understand it as meaning "Oh hurrah! Nest-egg pouched! TENNY." Let us pass hastily over this lapse from dignity, pausing only to admire the characteristically keen appreciation of Nature which the metaphor shows. And, indeed, the recognition was not undeserved, for it appears that the whole conception of the artifice originated with Tennyson: so at least the eighth cryptogram gives us to understand. "And leave the cliffs, and haste away" can hardly stand for anything but "La! What a safe device Alf had! TENNYS." He had indeed burrowed deep, but he should not have trusted to the impenetrability of his armour so far as to give way to these regrettable outbursts of exultation.

What, then, was the original purpose of the poem? Queen Victoria did not know Arthur Hallam, and it is clear that the initials were merely chosen in order to lend plausibility to the story that it was Tennyson's work. Was it then, some quite imaginary person whose death evoked this touching threnody? We might have remained in the dark, were it not for one final disclosure of the cypher-lines. The ninth cryptogram is more difficult to read than the others, because more allusively expressed, but there can be no doubt of the true version. "Nor, what may count itself as blest" must be "Let A.H. act for W. Lamb's suit. TENNYSO"—or possibly "Let W. Lamb suit, cast for A. H. TENNYSO." The metaphor will be sartorial on the former supposition, histrionic on the latter; in any case there can be no doubt as to the hero. William Lamb was the family name of that Lord Melbourne who was Queen Victoria's first and favorite Prime Minister. Mr. Lytton Strachey has given abundant evidence of the warm respect and admiration, something half filial and half romantic, which the young Queen felt for Lord Melbourne. When did he die? In the November of 1848, a date which exactly suits the circumstances of the poem. It enhances our respect for Queen Victoria's poetic gifts when we reflect that this long and intricate work was the fruit of little more than a year's labor.

The tenth cryptogram raises the question—If Victoria was the authoress of the poem, how was it that Tennyson came to supply the cypher? There must, it seems, have been collaboration here, and there could be few more generous tributes than that which is paid in the words "Such splendid purpose in his eyes." For these, when read, according to the cryptographer's intention, give you: "She lisp'd in sinuous cyphers deep"—the praise is the praise of Victoria, but the voice is the voice of Tennyson. And yet the man who could write such a line as that could take pride in signing himself at the conclusion of his cryptographic message: "A potent voice of Parliament," which, it need hardly be pointed out, stands for "Alf, poet-pen to Victoria. Amen."

The chain of evidence, then, may be summed up as follows:

1.	1	Who is writing this? H.M. luteth hid.
3.	2	V.R.I. the poetess. Alf T. has no duties.
6.	3	Pie hoc nomen clam commodans. T.
13.	4	Her Maiesty lacks pelf; I'le help. TE.
9.	5	O Mother, I'm H.M.'s shadow-author! TEN.
20.	6	Who pummels Faith-Defender? TENN.
41.	7	Oh, hurrah! Nest-egg pouched! TENNY.
12.	8	La! What a safe device Alf had! TENNYSO.
27.	I	Let A.H. act for W. Lamb suit. TENNYSO.
56.	10	She lisp'd in sinuous cyphers deep.
113.	11	Alf, poet-pen to Victoria. Amen.

There is much, no doubt, still to be explained as to the personal allusions of *In Memoriam:* some, no doubt, deliberately put in as a blind, others referring in a veiled way to incidents in Lord Melbourne's career. But, in the face of evidence such as this, will anyone attempt to rack the long arm of coincidence so as to make it cover this extraordinary series of cryptograms? If so, he has the ostrich-mind that cannot, because it will not, acquiesce in the assured results of modern enquiry.

Why Shakespeare more than anybody else?

—RONALD A. KNOX

Note: Knox wrote this as a spoof of the "higher criticism" of the Bible and of Shakespeare. Editor.

298

A *Letter in Cipher That Saved a Man's Life*

In England during the days of Cromwell, Sir John Trevanion, a cavalier of some distinction, was a prisoner in Colchester Castle awaiting execution. Upon receiving the following letter Sir John read it and read it and finally was enabled by it to make his escape:

> Worthy Sir John: Hope, that is the best comfort of the afflicted, cannot much, I fear me, help me now. That I would say to you, is this only, if ever I may be to requite that I do owe you, stand not upon asking me. 'Tis not much that I can do; but what I can do, bee you very sure I will. I know that, if death comes, if ordinary men fear it, it frights not you, accounting it for a high honor, to have such a reward of your loyalty. Pray yet that you may be spared this so bitter, cup. I fear not that you will grudge any sufferings; only if by submission you can turn them away, 'tis the part of a wise man. Tell me, an if you can, to do for you anything that you would have done. The general goes back on Wednesday. Resting your servant to command.— R. T.

Sir John decoded this message and was informed thru it: PANEL AT EAST END OF CHAPEL SLIDES.

He found this out by reading the third letter after each punctuation.

Cypher Verse

U O a O but I O U,
O O no O but O O me;
O let not my O a O go,
But give O O I O U so.

which means

You sigh for a cypher, but I sigh for you;
O sigh for no cypher, but O sigh for me;
O let not my sigh for a cypher go,
But give sigh for sigh, for I sigh for you so.

—WILLIAM WHEWELL

A Clergyman's Announcement to His Mother

From sweet Isaiah's sacred song, ninth chapter and
    verse six,
First thirteen words please take, and the following
    affix:
From Genesis, the thirty-fifth, verse seventeen, no
    more,
Then add verse twenty-six of Kings, book second, chap-
    ter four;
The last two verses, chapter first, first Book of Samuel,
And you will learn, what on that day, your loving son
    befell.

Following these directions the message as revealed by
the Bible is:

> For unto us a child is born, unto us
> a son is given. . . . And it came to pass,
> when she was in hard labour, that the
> midwife said unto her, Fear not; thou
> shalt have this son also. . . . Run now,
> I pray thee, to meet her; and say unto
> her, Is it well with thee? Is it well with
> thy husband? Is it well with the child?
> And she answered, It is well. . . . For
> this child I prayed, and the Lord hath
> given me my petition which I asked of
> him.
> Therefore also have I lent him to the
> Lord: as long as he liveth he shall be
> lent to the Lord. And he worshipped the
> Lord there.

And he spake to his sons, saying, Saddle me the ass. And they saddled *him*.

—I Kings 14:27

Then the angel of the Lord went forth, and smote in the camp of the Assyrians a hundred and four score and five thousand: and when they arose early in the morning, behold, they were all dead corpses.

—Isaiah 37:36

Samuel Foote, dramatist, devised the following as a challenge to one who boasted he could learn anything by heart after one reading of it:

So she went into the garden to cut a cabbage-leaf to make an apple pie and at the same time, a great she-bear coming up the street pops its head into the shop—What! no soap? So he died, and she very imprudently married the barber; and there were present the Picinnies, and the great Panjandrum himself, with the little round button at the top. And they all fell playing the game of "catch as catch can," till the gunpowder ran out of the heels of their boots!

What Do We Forget?

If a man says that he forgets what he does not wish to remember, does he mean to say that he does not remember what it is that he wishes to forget, or that he is able to forget that which he does not wish to remember?

"I quite agree with you," said the Duchess, "and the moral of that is—'Be what you would seem to be'— or if you'd like it put more simply—Never imagine yourself not to be otherwise than what it might appear to others that that what you were or might have been was not otherwise than what you had been would have appeared to them to be otherwise."

—LEWIS CARROLL

"Take some more tea," the March Hare said to Alice, very earnestly.

"I've had nothing yet," Alice replied in an offended tone, "so I couldn't take more."

"You mean you can't take less," said the Hatter; "It's very easy to take *more* than nothing."

—LEWIS CARROLL

"How long does this train stop here" a woman passenger asked the trainman.

"Two to two to two-two," he replied.

"The poor man," mused the lady; "he must be out of his mind and think that he is a locomotive."

Epitaph on William More

Here lies one *More*, and *no* more than he!
One More and *no more!* how can that be?
Why *one More* and *no more*, may lie here alone;
But here lies one *More*, and that's *more* than one!
                 (Stepney Church-yard, England)

Tavern Talk

At a tavern one night,
Messieurs More, Strange and Wright,
Met to drink, and good thoughts to exchange;
  Says More, "Of us three,
  The whole town will agree
There is only one knave, and that's Strange."
  "Yes," says Strange (rather sore),
  "I am sure there's one More,
A most terrible knave and a bite;
  Who cheated his mother,
  Sister and brother."
"O yes," replied More, "that is Wright."

—John Philpot Curran

Gobbledygook

A doctor testified at an English trial that one of the parties was suffering from "circumorbital haematoma." That is, a black eye.

In August, 1952, the U. S. Department of Agriculture published a pamphlet titled: *Cultural and Pathogenic Variability in Single-Condial and Hyphaltip Isolates of Hemlin-Thosporium Turcicum Pass.*
This proved to be about corn-leaf disease.

When he reached the top of the Finsteraarhorn in 1845, one M. Dollfus-Ausset exclaimed: "The soul communes in the infinite with those icy peaks which seem to have their roots in the bowels of eternity."
—STUART CHASE

Clifford B. Reeves, an insurance executive, collects what he calls "bafflegab" and gives this as one instance:

> One-half to his mother, if living, if not to his father, and one-half to his mother-in-law, if living, if not to his mother, if living, if not to his father. Thereafter payment is to be made in a single sum to his brothers. On the one-half to his mother, if living, if not to his father, he does not bring in his mother-in-law as the next payee to receive, although on the one-half to his mother-in-law, he does bring in the mother or father.
>
> (in interview with Sylvia Porter)

Confusion Compounded

"I am terribly disturbed," said a young woman to her friend. "I wrote Reginald in my last letter to forget that I told him I didn't mean to reconsider my decision not to change my mind—and he seems to have misunderstood me."

She never says a kind word, and when she does, she doesn't mean it.

I'll never forget you until the day you die, if you should live so long.
—W. W. FEARNSIDE AND W. B. HOLTHER

Why, I see you are here first at last. You were always behind before, but I am glad to see you have become early of late.

One way to end a letter: Give everybody's love to everybody, so that nobody may be aggrieved by anybody being forgotten by somebody.

A newspaper reporter asked a politician: "Mr. Jones, you may recall that our paper printed last week your denial of having retracted the contradiction of your original statement. Now, would you care to have us say that you were misquoted in regard to it?"

In response to a reporter's question, Abraham Lincoln said: "I fear explanations explanatory of things explained."

I cannot bear to see a bear, bear down upon a hare.
When bare of hair he strips the hare,
For hare I cry "Forebear!"

I saw Esau kissing Kate,
And the fact is we all three saw;
For I saw Esau, he saw me,
And she saw I saw Esau.

The Careful Penman
A Persian named Aziz,
Remarked, "I think I know my biz,
For when I write my name as is,
It is Aziz as is Aziz."

Echoes

What must be done to conduct a newspaper right?
Write.

What is necessary for a farmer to assist him? System.

What would give a blind man the greatest delight?
Light.

What is the best counsel given by a justice of the
peace? Peace.

Who commits the greatest abominations? Nations.

What cry is the greatest terrifier? Fire.

What are some of women's chief exercise? Sighs.

Spoonerisms

Reverend W. A. Spooner (1844-1930) was famous for his habitual metathesis—the transposition of the initial sounds of words so as to form some laughable combination. Some of the best perpretrated by, or at least attributed to, the Warden of New College, Oxford, are:

Upon dismissing a student: "You have deliberately tasted two worms; you can leave Oxford by the town drain."

"We all know what it is to have a half-warmed fish within us" (for "half-formed wish").

"Yes, indeed, the Lord is a shoving leopard."

He once asked a waitress for "a glass bun and and a bath of milk."

Rebuking his congregation for its small attendance and meaning to refer to the "weary benches," he said: "I am tired of addressing these beery wenches."

"Sir, I believe you are under the affluence of incohol."

"Now Rabbabbas was a bobber."

He referred to a "blushing crow" instead of a "crushing blow."

"It is kisstomary to cuss the bride."

And perhaps most famous of all, he said: "Mardon me, Padam, but I am afraid that you are occupewing the wrong pie. May I sew you to another sheet?"

YY UR, YY U B, I C U R YY 4 ME means: "Too wise
you are, too wise you be: I see you are too wise for me."

EEE & XXX URXXI; XXX & eee means: "Great ease
and small crosses before you are twenty-one; great
crosses and little ease after that."

ALLO means: "Nothing after all."

$$\frac{C}{T\ T\ T\ T\ T\ T\ T\ T\ T\ T}$$

T T T T T T T T T T means: "Contents" (C on ten
Ts).

INXINXIN means: "Ink sinks in."

4A. 80 means: "For a period I ate next to nothing."

This is Hogarth's picture of a soldier and his dog going
through a doorway.

OVER
STANDING   TOWERING MAN JUDGES MAN
AN   MIND
means: "An understanding and overtowering mind
judges between man and man."

If the B m t put: but if the B. putting: can be translated to: "If the grate be empty put coal on; but if the grate be full, stop putting coal on."

LOOK
LOOK U LOOK
LOOK
AND
C THAT O VXS NOR XX UR II

means: "Look around you always, and see that nothing vexes nor crosses your eyes."

WE WESTAND FALL means: "United we stand, divided we fall."

I AM
A MAN
I RATE YOU
A BEAST
YOU KNOW ME

means: "I rate you lower than a man, above a beast; know between you and me I am above the rest."

MARIGARE stands for "mixed Marriage."

DKI stands for "mixed-up kid."

CCC
SAW

means: The season was backward (The C's on WAS backward).

"ABCDQTT?"
"OMNOQTT."
"OSARABCM?"
"OGICMSAR
LNLC&LOEE!"

means: "Abie, see de cuties?"
"Oh, 'em ain' no cuties."
"Oh, 'es, 'ey are, Abie, see 'em?"
"Oh, gee, I see 'em; 'es, 'ey are Ellen, Elsie and Eloise!"

A man found the following on a post down South:

TOTI
EMUL
ESTO

and while examining it and wondering about it asked a farm boy its meaning. "Oh, my Pappy put that there," the boy said. "If you stop after the second letter and the fifth letter and then the tenth letter, you'll see what it means: 'To Ties Mules To.'"

—CHARLES FRANCIS POTTER

STAND   TAKE   TO   TAKING
I   YOU   THROW   MY

means: "I understand you undertake to overthrow my undertaking."

B
FAULTS MAN QUARRELS WIFE FAULTS
means: "Be above quarrels between man and wife; there are faults on both sides."

NEWS, it has been suggested, derives from the first letters of the four directions: North, East, West, South.

STORM   AN UMBRELLA   WITH   ALL
A TH   ME WHO   ALLS   MUD

means: "Who follows me under an umbrella, with overalls all over mud, after a thunderstorm."

S P A C E   stands for "wide-open spaces."

L E G A L   stands for "legal separation."

FAR   HOME   stands for "far away from home."

RE–RE stands for "repaired."

BANGFF means "starting off with a bang."

WOWOLFOL stands for "wolf in sheep's clothing."

DLIHC stands for "backward child."

RAC is "a car in reverse."

GNIKOOL means "looking backward."

—EVAN ESAR

A letter addressed as follows:

> Wood,
> John,
> Mass.

was properly delivered to:

> John Underwood,
> Andover, Mass.

Apt Anagrams

The letters comprising the words or phrases in the left-hand column, when rearranged, form the words or phrases in the right-hand column.

ASTRONOMERS	NO MORE STARS, or MOON-STARERS
ELEGANT	NEAT LEG
LAWYERS	SLY WARES
PUNISHMENT	NINE THUMPS
PENITENTIARY	NAY, I REPENT IT
RADICAL REFORM	RARE MAD FROLIC
REVOLUTION	TO LOVE RUIN
PARADISE REGAINED	DEAD RESPIRE AGAIN
PARLIAMENT	PARTIAL MEN
SOVEREIGNTY	'TIS YE GOVERN
HYSTERICS	HIS SET CRY
IRELAND	ERIN LAD
MATRIMONY	INTO MY ARMS
MATRIMONIALS	O, I'M MAN'S TRIAL
PARADISE LOST	REAP SAD TOIL
POORHOUSE	O SOUR HOPE!
ALFRED TENNYSON	FANS ONE TENDERLY
WILLIAM SHAKESPEARE	I SWEAR HE IS LIKE A LAMP, or I ASK ME, HAS WILL A PEER?
FRENCH REVOLUTION	VIOLENCE RUN FORTH
IS PITY LOVE?	POSITIVELY
FLORENCE NIGHTINGALE	CLING ON, FEELING HEART
CHRISTIANITY	I CRY THAT I SIN
FUNERAL	REAL FUN
THE CLASSROOM	SCHOOLMASTER

SAINTS	STAINS
LEPER	REPEL
PARISHIONERS	I HIRE PARSONS
MIDSHIPMAN	MIND HIS MAP
SURGEON	GO! NURSE!
UNITED STATES	IN TE DEUS STAT (God stands in thee)
CRINOLINE	INNER COIL
DETERMINATION	I MEAN TO REND IT
PRESBYTERIAN	BEST IN PRAYER
NAPOLEON BONAPARTE	NO, APPEAR NOT AT ELBA
SWEETHEART	THERE WE SAT
UNCONVENTIONALITIES	UNITE IN NOVEL ACTIONS
HIBERNATE	THE BEAR IN
IMPATIENT	TIM IN A PET
GALLANTRIES	ALL GREAT SIN
MONARCH	MARCH ON
OLD ENGLAND	GOLDEN LAND
DEMOCRATICAL	COMICAL TRADE
JAMES WATT	WAIT, STEAM, and A STEAM WIT
THE MIDNIGHT RIDE OF PAUL REVERE	RIDER GAVE HINT OF PERIL DUE
A. HITLER	THE LIAR
PORTERHOUSE	OUR PET HORSE
CENSUS ENUMERATORS	HE'S A TRUE MEN'S COUNTER

ARTHUR WELLESLEY, DUKE OF WELLINGTON (who led the forces that defeated Napoleon at Waterloo) may be transposed to LET WELL FAIL'D GAUL SECURE THY RENOWN.

Has there been a poet of unusual SOLEMNITY? YES, MILTON.

In word and WILL I AM a friend to you;
And one friend OLD is worth a hundred new.

—WILLIAM OLDY

Anagram on THOMAS PARRE, of Shropshire, buried in the south transept of Westminster Abbey in 1635, at the age of 152 and 9 months: MOST RARE HAP

If you transpose what ladies wear—VEIL,
'Twill plainly show what bad folks are—VILE.

Again, if you transpose the same,
You'll see an ancient Hebrew name—LEVI.

Change it again and it will show
What all on earth desire to do—LIVE.

Transpose the letters yet once more,
What bad men do you'll then explore—EVIL.

Politicians' names are bound to be anagrammatized. For example:

THEODORE ROOSEVELT	HERO, TOLD TO OVERSEE
GROVER CLEVELAND	GOVERN, CLEVER LAD
DWIGHT D. EISENHOWER	WOW! HE'S RIGHT INDEED!

FRANKLIN DELANO ROOSEVELT, when he ran against Alf Landon for the Presidency in 1936, was changed by a Landon supporter, to VOTE FOR LANDON, ERE ALL SINK.

Dmitri A. Borgmann, of Oak Park, Illinois, suggested that LYNDON BAINES JOHNSON could be changed by the Democrats to NO NINNY, HE'S ON JOB LADS,

322

and by the Republicans to HA, NOD ON, JOBLESS NINNY, for use upon his retirement from office.

Mr. Borgmann, an avid linguistic manipulator, changed HALITOSIS into LOIS HAS IT and SPUTNIK into IT'S PUNK. He suggests that MEDICAL CONSULTATIONS could be changed into NOTED MISCALCULATIONS, casting modesty aside, rearranges his own name, DMITRI ALFRED BORGMANN into GRAND MIND, MORTAL FIBRE.

An extraordinary anagram is found in the Latin of Pilate's question to Jesus: QUID EST VERITAS? (What is truth?). Rearranged, the question contains its own answer: EST VIR QUI ADEST (It is the man who is before you).

Acrostic

Unite and untie are the same—so say yoU
Not in wedlock, I ween, has this unity beeN.
In the drama of marriage each wandering gouT
To a new face would fly—all except you and I—
Each seeking to alter the *spell* in their scenE.

Palindromes

Though remote from glittering prose, there is an odd kind of amusement to be derived from the following sentence:

Nan the *nun* told *Anna* at *noon* to *repaper* the *radar* on the *poop* deck of the *kayak*, and to *refer Otto* to the *reviver* on the *rotator* so that *Hannah* and *Ada* and *Eve* on the *gig* keep an *eye* on the *civic tenet* and do not *peep* the deed done *Aba* and *Bab by Pop, Sis*, and the *pup*.

Now, if you look back you will discover—if you have not already—that each italicized word reads the same forward and backward. They are palindromes—from the Greek *palin drome,* "to turn back again."

Perhaps the sentence could be made longer—and sillier—by adding a few more palindromes, such as pap, pip, tot, bib, ewe, gag, solos, sexes, tat, Anana, minim, sees, toot, boob.

More intriguing, however, are sentence palindromes, such as Napoleon's imaginary remark, "Able was I ere I saw Elba," or "Live was I ere I saw evil." "Madam, I'm Adam" is equally famous, with its variation of "Madam! I mad—am I, Madam?"

A few more sentence palindromes are:

Draw pupil's lip upward.
A man, a plan, a canal—Panama.
Are we not drawn onward, we few, drawn onward to new era?
Snug and raw was I ere I saw war and guns.
Dog as a devil deified, deified lives as a god.
Paget saw an Irish tooth, sir, in a waste gap.
Dennis and Edna sinned.
Ma is a nun, as I am.
Sums are not set as a test on Erasmus.
Niagara, O roar again!

"Rats live on no evil star" is a rather less popular palindrome. But then we have "Rise to vote, sir" and "Name no one man" which are fairly commonplace remarks one might not suspect as being palindromes. And the question "Was it a cat I saw?" has been given a palindrome answer: "No, Miss, it's Simon."

On the other hand, "Stop Rose, I prefer pies or pots," "Live on no evil," "Egad, a base tone denotes a bad age," and "Eve damned Eden, mad Eve!" might well invite one to take a closer look at their construction.

The true palindrome is from letter to letter, as in the ones already given. Less difficult, but still amusing, are the word-to-word palindromes, such as:

> Hand that saw to saw that hand.
> Love your treasure and treasure your love.
> Work for money as well as money for work.
> You provoked Mary before Mary provoked you.
> Row Black beyond Black Row.

Though not palindromes, the following are in the same genre since they retain the same meaning when read backwards:

> Dies slowly fading day, winds mournful sigh,
> Brightly stars are waking;
> Flies owlet hooting, holding revel high,
> Nightly silence breaking.

> ### A DOCTOR'S ADVICE
> Play with work blend, keep warmish feet,
> Away drive trouble, slowly eat;
> Air pure breathe and early rise,
> Beware excess, take exercise.

It is easier, of course, to bring off the same result in a single sentence:

Scandalous society and life make gossips frantic.
Badly governed and fearfully troubled now's Ireland.
Carefully boiled eggs are good and palatable.

She sits lamenting sadly, often too much alone.
Man is noble and generous often, but sometimes vain and
cowardly.

But to upset the whole palindrome business, here is a gloomy forecast that is changed to a cheerful prophesy when read in reverse:

Comes Christmas merry? Hungry birds; no bright berries;
Rents high, not paid; long bills; empty barns, no peace and
prosperity.

Prosperity and peace; no barns empty; bills long paid;
Not high rents; berries bright; no birds hungry merry Christmas comes.

Word expert William Morris refers to the recently developed mathematical or numerical palindrome—numbers that can be read rightside up and upside down, such as 0890. 1991 will be the next palindrome year. 1881 and 1961 read the same when held upside down, and 1881 remains the same when held up to a mirror.

Five words which, when capitalized, read the same forward, backward and when held to a mirror are:

TOOT   NOON   WOW   MOM   TOT   OTTO

Talented Martin Gardner refers to words that become different words when reversed as a semordnilap, or palindromes reversed. As examples he cites:

LIVE   STRAW   DESSERTS   REDRAWER

Mrs. Kathryn Akin came up recently with a name for palindromes which read the same upside down, such as NOON. It's a jawbreaker: *aufdenkopfstellenumgekehrt*—a German word meaning "on the head standing in reverse."

Hallam's Famous Unsolved Enigma

I sit on a rock while I'm raising the wind,
But the storm once abated I'm gentle and kind.
I've kings at my feet, who await but my nod
To kneel in the dust on the ground I have trod.
Though seen to the world, I am known to but few.
The Gentiles detest me, I'm pork to the Jews.

I never have passed but one night in the dark,
And that was with Noah alone in the Ark,
My weight is three pounds, my length is a mile.
And when I'm discovered you'll say with a smile,
That my first and my last are the pride of this isle.

Apparently no one has given a completely satisfactory solution to this enigma. RAVEN has been offered
as the answer because it croaks before a storm, was
once an object of worship, is seldom seen, is forbidden
in Leviticus as food, was alone with Noah in the Ark
when its mate was sent forth, weighs about three
pounds, is the name of a small South Carolina island,
and its first and last initial, stand for Royal Navy.

Five simple letters do compose my frame;
And, what is singular, when viewed, my name
Forwards and backwards will be found the same.
When I'm discovered, you will plainly see
What the proud seer and peasant soon will be.*
* LEVEL

What Is It?

The beginning of eternity, the end of time and space,
The beginning of every end, and the end of every
place.*

* *The letter* E

Tipperary

A certain Dr. Fitzgerald wrote a poem upon his native Tipperary that ends:

> And thou dear village, loveliest of the clime,
> Fain would I name thee, but I scan't in rhyme.

He was answered in the following fashion by an anonymous wag:

> A poet there was in a sad quandry,
> To find a rhyme for Tipperary.
> Long labored he through January,
> Yet found no rhyme for Tipperary;
> Toiled every day in February,
> But toiled in vain for Tipperary;
> Searched Hebrew text and commentary,
> But searched in vain for Tipperary;
> Bored all his friends in Inverary,
> To find a rhyme for Tipperary;
> Implored the aid of "Paddy Cary,"
> Yet still no rhyme for Tipperary;
> He next besought his mother Mary
> To tell him rhyme for Tipperary;
> But she, good woman, was no fairy,
> Nor witch—though born in Tipperary;
> Knew everything about her dairy,
> But not the rhyme for Tipperary;
> The stubborn muse he could not vary,
> For still the lines would run contrary
> When'er he thought on Tipperary.
> And though of time he was not chary,

'Twas thrown away on Tipperary.
Till of his wild-goose chase most weary,
He vowed he'd leave out Tipperary.
But no—the theme he might not vary,
His longing was not temporary,
To find meet rhyme for Tipperary.
He sought among the gay and airy,
He pestered all the military.
Committed many a strange vagary,
Bewitched, it seems, by Tipperary.
He wrote, post-haste, to Darby Leary,
Besought with tears his Auntie Sairy;
But sought he far, or sought he near, he
Ne'er found a rhyme for Tipperary.
He traveled sad through Cork and Kerry,
He drove like mad through sweet Dunleary,
Kicked up a precious tantar-ara,
But found no rhyme for Tipperary;
Lived fourteen weeks at Stan-ar-ara,
Was well-nigh lost in Glenegary,
Then started slick for Demerara,
In search of rhyme for Tipperary.
Through Yankee-land, sick, solitary,
He roamed by forest, lake and prairie,
He went *per terram et par mare*,
But found no rhyme for Tipperary.
Through Orient climes on dromedary,
On camel's back through great Sahara;
His travels were extraordinary
In search of rhyme for Tipperary.
Fierce as a gorgon or chimaera,
Fierce as Alecto or Megaera,
Fiercer than e'er a love-sick bear, he
Ranged through the londe of Tipperary.
His cheeks grew thin and wondrous hairy,

His visage long, his aspect eerie;
His *tout ensemble,* faith, would scare ye,
Amidst the wilds of Tipperary.
Becoming hypochon-dri-ary,
He sent for his apothecary,
Who ordered "balm and saponary,"
Herbs rare to find in Tipperary.
In his potations ever wary,
His choicest drink was "home goose-berry."
On swipes, skim-milk and smallest beer, he
Scanted rhymes for his Tipperary.
Had he imbibed good Madeira,
Drank bottle-deep of golden sherry,
Of Falstaff's sack, or ripe Canary,
No rhyme had lacked for Tipperary.
Or had his tastes been literary,
He might have found extemporary
Without the aid of dictionary,
Some fitting rhyme for Tipperary.
Or had he been an antiquary,
Burnt midnight oil in his library,
Or been of temper less "camstary,"
Rhymes had not lacked for Tipperary.
He paced about his aviary,
Blew up, sky-high, his secretary,
And then in wrath and anger sware he,
There was no rhyme for Tipperary.

Index of Authors,

Subjects, and Titles

Accountants Can't Agree On This, 229
Achilles and the Tortoise, 3
Acrostic, 324
Adam's Navel, 151
Akin, Kathryn, 327
Alice in Wonderland, 80–81, 283, 306
Almanach of Gotha, 237
Anagrams, 320–323
Andrei Bumblowski's Dream Experience in Hell, 157–159
Angels On Head of a Pin, 154
Apples Eaten by Adam and Eve, 198
Appraisals, Method of, 230
Arabin, Serjeant, 280
Are Parents Murderers?, 84
Aristotle, 21, 150, 162, 172, 175
Aroo, King, 47
Athiest's Sign, 289
Ausubel, Nathan, 118–119
Authorship of *In Memoriam*, 291–298
Aziz, 312

Bafflegab, 310
Bagehot, Walter, 184–185
Baker, Frank, 231
Bank Deposit, 213
Barataria, Island of, 63
Barber, Shaving the, 42
Bargain, 191
Barnum, P. T., 242

Beggar and the Buns, The, 245
Begging the Question, 129
Bernard, Tristan, 271
Biblical Bulls, 302
Bill Collecting, 217
Blough, Roger, 215
Blumenthal, Walter Hart, 270–271
Boccaccio, 66
Borgmann, Dmitri, 322–323
Brennecke, Ernest, 269
Browne, Sir Thomas, 151
Brussel's World's Fair, 223
Bulls: Irish and Others, 279–280, 302

Cabot, Richard C., 74
Carey, Henry, 262
Carroll, Lewis, 6, 13, 30, 69, 72, 80–81, 101–102, 103, 116, 155, 210, 214, 273, 283, 305, 306
Cash, 172
Caught Again, 99
Cervantes, Miguel de, 27, 63–64
Chase, Stuart, 310
Check That Didn't Bounce, The, 217
Christianity: Calculating Date of Its Demise, 235
Chrysippus, 20, 149
Chuang Tzŭ, 52, 82, 142
Cicero, 149, 153
Circular Economy, 225
Cleinias, 136, 143, 169

Clergyman's Announcement to His Mother, 301
Clever Missionary, The, 23
Coal Deliveries, 196
Cohen, Morris R., 141
Colchester Castle, 299
Coleridge, Samuel Taylor, 49
Compound Words, Satirizing Users of, 262
Computer Confusion, 278
Concealed Deer, The, 50
Confusion Compounded, 311
Conjugations, 268
Consoling Analysis, 239
Contradiction, 91, 166, 169–170, 171
Contradiction, Proving Impossibility of, 169–170
Correlation, 92
Could the Earth Run Backward?, 76
Crane, Burton, 248
Cretans, 20, 21
Cryptography, 291–298, 299
Ctesippus, 135, 169, 173
Curran, John Philpot, 309
Cutting a Cake, 65
Cynics, 138
Cypher Verse, 300

D'Albert, Jean, 152
Damning a Man When He Does and When He Does Not, 136–137
Day Defined, 72
Death, How to Defeat, 36
Death, Proving the Non-Existence of, 35, 164
Deduction, 115, 117
De Morgan, Augustus, 17, 39, 48, 142, 235
De Quincey, Thomas, 11–12, 21, 53
Determinism, 188
Dialogue in Two Words, 276

Did Nott Shoot Shott?, 277
Diodorus the Megaric, 144
Diogenes, 7
Diogenes Laertes, 20, 108
Dionysodorus, 135, 136, 169, 173
Divisibility, Infinite, 3–6, 147
Donato, Pietro di, 79
Do-Nothing Fallacy, The, 153
Dream Dilemmas, 48–54, 238
Drinking, Rules for, 284

Echoes, 313
Eddington, A. S., 114
Elizabeth, Queen, 282
Emerson, Ralph Waldo, 201
Epicurus, 38
Epimenides, 20, 21
Epitaphs, 33–34, 308
Equivocation, 282, 284, 285, 311
Esar, Evan, 106, 318
Esau, 312
Euathlos, 46
Euclid, 11
Euthydemus, 136, 173
Evershamen, S., 206
Existence, 141, 142, 156, 164, 177, 182
Experience, 197

Fallacy of the Heap, 149, 150
Fallacy of Many Questions, 105
False Opinion Has No Existence, 139
Famous Question, 171
Fearnside, W. W., 47, 107, 109, 311
Fifty-Cent Barrel of Whiskey, The, 191
Finan, James, 200
Find the Liar, 22
Fishes, Pleasures of, 82

336

Folly of Rationalization in Advance of Experience, 114
Foote, Samuel, 303
Fraser, J. T., 77
Freedom, 184–185
Free Will, 188
Fun Raiser, A, 207

Gamow, George, 15
Gardner, Martin, 117, 327
Geographical Question, 17
Gilbert, W. S., 112
Giles, H. A., 50–51
Globe-Circling, 60
Gobbledygook, 310
God, Omnipotence of, 37
Going Round the Squirrel, 61–62
Gomperz, 21
Good Does Not Exist, 167
Gorgias, 177
Government Regulations, Nazi, 218
Gray, Thomas, 272
Greenblatt, M. H., 23–24, 28, 246, 278
Grosseteste, Robert, 180
Guitry, Sacha, 109
Gupta, S. N., 166

Hallam's Unsolved Enigma, 328
Hamilton, Sir William, 4
Happiness Is Impossible, 165
Hartmann, Edward von, 182
Hell, 157–159
Hempel's Paradox, 28
Herophilus, 144
Hilbert, David, 15
Hodgson, S. H., 67
Hogarth, 315
Holther, W. B., 107, 109, 311
Homer, 10

Horse, selection of by Arab chieftain, 58
Horse Trade, 246
How Old Is Anne?, 232
How to Please Industry, 216
Huck Finn, 93
Huff, Darrell, 208
Hui Tzŭ, 82, 147
Hunt, Leigh, 286

Inference, 82
Infinite, 4, 13, 15, 83, 145, 176
Infinite Hotel, 15
Ingenious Ignoramus, 118–119
Investing, 201–204
Irresistible Force vs. Immovable Object, 171
Is Man a False God?, 180

James, William, 61–62, 67
Johnson, Burges, 222
Johnson, Wendell, 154
Jourdain, P. E. B., 20, 186
Jowett, Benjamin, 131

Kasner, Edward, 56, 60
Kent, Jack, 47
Kingsley, Charles, 263
Knowledge, Decline and Revival of, 155
Knox, Ronald A., 291–298
Koestler, Arthur, 19

Labor, 216
Lamb, Charles, 234
Leacock, Stephen, 192–194
Legal Dilemmas, 46, 59
Le Win, R. Arnold, 249
Liar Sophism, The, 20–21
Lie, No One Can Tell a, 173
Light, Speed of, 76, 78
Lincoln, Abraham, 311
Long Words, 263, 264

337

Lo! the Poor Foreman, 79
Lost Chord, The, 192–194
Lottery Winner, 238
Lovell, a Naturalist, 263

Macmurray, John, 188
McTaggert, Mc. T. E., 43
Maharajah of Lahore, 237
Man Who Climbed the Mountain, The, 19
Man Who Meets His Younger-Self, The, 75
Marriage-Age Differentials, 195, 224
Mascall, E. L., 188
Mathematic of the Lost Chord, 192–194
Meaning, 186, 283
Memorizing, 303, 304
Metaphysical Question, 160
Mill, John Stuart, 4–5
Mississippi River, The, 247
Mitchell, Edward Page, 70–71
Molyneux, William, 18
Moment, 67–68
Monday Drunkards, The, 11–12
Moore, G. E., 181
More, William, Epitaph on, 308
Morris, William, 327
Moscow Radio, 231
Mother and Crocodile Debate, 44
Motion, 3, 7, 8, 9, 144
Mousetrap Myth, The, 201–204
Munchausen, Baron, 25
Mysterious Message, 26

Names of Children, 281
Navel Battle, 151
Nazis, 218
Newman, James, 5–6, 60
New Statesman, The, 268

Nothing, 157–159, 163, 177, 181

Orleton, Bishop Adam de, 270
Oursler, Fulton, 90

Palindromes, 325–327
Palmerston, Lord, 267
Parental Common Sense, 111
Pascal, Blaise, 251
Past, The, Can It Be Changed?, 73
Paul, St., 20
Pavlovic, Sam, 207
Pepper, Claude, 284
Peripatetics, 146
Philetas, 20
Philoponus, 145
Philosopher Defined, 152
Philosophical Puzzle, 156
Place Does Not Exist, 145, 146
Plato, 135, 136–137, 139–140, 143, 169–170, 173–174
Plutarch, 10
Poetical Shorthand, 286
Polynyms, 288
Population Explosion Exploded, 237
Potter, Charles Francis, 316
Present Moment, The, 67–68
Priestley, J. B., 73, 76
Private Judgment, 121
Problem of Evil, The, 38
Prochnow, Herbert V., 29
Profit, Margin of, 236
Pronunciations, 263–266
Prospectus Lacon, Ill., Cat-and-Rat Ranch, 211
Protagoras, 46, 150
Proving a Man's Dog Is His Father, 135
Public Affairs, Engaging in, 175

Punctuation, 268, 269, 270, 271, 272

Reader's Digest, 260–261
Reality, 181
Rebuses, 315–319
Reeves, Clifford B., 310
Reichenbach, Hans, 75
Rejecting Argument That Cannot Be Refuted, 178
Relative Problems, 29–34
Relativity, 248
Reversibility of Time, 77
Ricardo, David, 216
Riddles, 10, 328–330
Right, 187
Ritchie of Edinburgh, Dr., 95
Roche, Sir Boyle, 279–280
Rosten, Leo, 265
Russell, Bertrand, 40–41, 55–56, 67–68, 78, 157–159
Russians, 223, 227, 231
Ryan, Michael, 99

Sancho Panza, 27, 63–64
Satan, 157–159
Scaliger, Joseph, 262
Schiller, F. C. S., 83, 84, 183, 197
Schnitzler, Arthur, 35
Science, 113, 114, 247–250
Scientific References, Imaginary, 249
Seeing, 55–56
Senior, Nassau, 216
Shakespeare, William, 264
Sextus Empiricus, 54, 146, 161, 164, 165, 167, 178
Shipley, Joseph T., 270, 274
Shortest Sentences Containing All Letters of Alphabet, 287
Shrinking River, The, 247
Simplicius, 4, 8
Slander, 239

Smathers, Congressman, 284
Socrates, 139, 143, 164
Sophist, 162
Sophistical Tricks, 123
Soul, Proof of, 179
Space, 13, 74, 75, 83
Spanish Inquisition, 168
Spelling, 265–267
Spencer, Herbert, 9, 166
Spinoza, Baruch, 188
Spooner, Rev. W. A., 314
Spoonerisms, 314
Stalin's Bier, 231
Standen, Anthony, 92
Statistical "Proof," 200
Statistics, 200, 208, 215
Sterne, Laurence, 40
Stewart, Balfour, 179
Stocking Puzzle, 16
Stork, The One-Legged, 66
Strong, Dr. Thomas Banks, 210
Stupidity Essential for Preservation of Freedom, 184–185
Successful Ignoramus, The, 236
Swift, Jonathan, 279
Syllogisms, 91, 94, 97, 105, 124–128, 130, 172, 175

Tabori, Paul, 237
Tait, Peter G., 179
Tavern Talk, 309
Taylor, Jeremy, 53
Taylor, Robert, 148
Tell, William, 276
Ten Boxes, The, 89
Tennyson, Alfred, 291–298
Theatetus, 139
Themistocles' Child, 97
Theological Question, 148
Thouless, R. H., 268
Three Barbers, The, 101–102
Time, 67–78, 120

339

Time-Order, 78
Tipperary, 331–333
Titus, 20
Tooke, Horne, 94
Topping the Teacher, 95
Touch and Sight, 18
Trade, 191, 236
Trading Tricks, 240–246
Transformations, 273
Translation, 270, 278
Trevanion, Sir John, 299
Tricking a Thief, 199
Tristram Shandy's Dilemma, 40–41
True Does Not Exist, The, 161
Truth, 161, 163, 183
Turncoats, 244
Twain, Mark, 93, 247
Two Clocks, The, 69

Unicorns, 181
Universal Solvent, 57
Universe, 83
Unknowable, The, 166

Verbal Victory, 223
Voliva, Wilbur Glenn, 250

Wages, Law of, 216

Welby, Lady Viola, 186
What Do We Forget?, 304
Whately, Richard, 121
When the Unreal Is Real, 181
Whewell, William, 300
Who Drinks the Water? Who Owns the Zebra?, 85–86
Who Paid for the Beer?, 212
Who's Ahead?, 227
Why Frenchmen Should Talk English, 93
Why God Is Not an Infinite Being, 176
Why Nothing Becomes, 177
Why Study?, 104
Why Truth Is True, 163
Why Work?, 205, 206
Why Worry?, 106
Will, Arab's, 246
Wisdom of Governor Sancho, 63–64
Woods, Ralph L., 201–204
Word Gallery, 261–262
Word-Square, Famous Latin, 275

Yankee Stratagems, 242

Zeno, 3, 7, 145, 150, 153